HOMO SAPIENS PART - XVIII

121 CONTEMPORARY VERSES FOR ADMIRERS OF POETRY

MAWPHNIANG NAPOLEON

To the poetry devotee, The striving soul -

Let these carefully curated verses remind you of our shared
human spirit.

May their timeless truths resonate, transport and nourish.

We dedicate this anthology to you, seeker of solace, champion of
empathy, admirer of beauty.

To all who find community in poetry's hallowed halls across ages
and cultures.

Napoleon gifts you this sublime collection, that it might lift your
gaze to our humanity's higher reaches.

.

.

.

With admiration and camaraderie,

.

.-The Homo Sapiens Series Team

Contents

Contents

Contents

Contents

Contents

Contents

Foreword

We are delighted to present the newest addition to Mawphniang Napoleon's celebrated Homo Sapiens anthology series - a thoughtfully curated collection of 121 contemporary poems entitled "Contemporary Verse for Admirers of Poetry."

This volume represents Napoleon's abiding love letter to the artform itself and to all who find truth, beauty, and community within poetry's hallowed halls. The selected works traverse continents, cultures and centuries - from Ancient Roman Stoic philosophizing to postmodern Surrealist experimentation. Yet each rings with the timeless joys, sorrows, curiosities, and quandaries that define our shared human spirit.

Napoleon's deft curation allows readers to transcend time and space, finding camaraderie and resonance across divides. Here, Romantic odes to passion and nature sit alongside cerebral meditations on existence. Those seeking profundity will find wisdom in the Stoic masters, while devotees of creative expression will delight in the rule-breaking Surrealists. In these pages, poetry's myriad forms all have a home.

It is our hope this thoughtfully compiled anthology will rekindle your love of verse. That you discover new favorite works to revisit and recite. And that Napoleon's selections remind you of poetry's enduring power to illuminate, nurture and connect. To provide solace, inspiration and community.

To all admirers of poetry's rich heritage, from the classics to the contemporary - this collection is lovingly dedicated to you. May you find within these poems familiar truths, transporting vistas, and your own humanity gazing back.

With admiration,

,
The Homo Sapiens Series Team

Preface

We are proud to unveil the latest addition to Mawphniang Napoleon's acclaimed Homo Sapiens anthology series - a compilation of 121 contemporary poems aptly titled "Contemporary Verse for Admirers of Poetry."

This volume represents a celebration of poetry itself and the diverse community of readers who find truth, solace and beauty within its lines. Napoleon has expertly curated works spanning continents, cultures and eras - each brimming with insight into the human spirit's endless capacities for wisdom, passion, despair and imagination.

Devout readers will discover old favorites as well as new gems to treasure. Epic effusions by Romantic masters mingle with postmodern Surrealist experimentation. The measured contemplations of Roman Stoics complement modern philosophical musings. Yet no matter the form, Napoleon unifies these works by their common aim - to illuminate the shared emotional landscape of humankind.

We hope Napoleon's thoughtful curation helps readers transcend divides and find camaraderie. That devotees of the classics gain new appreciation for the avant-garde. And that those immersed in the contemporary find resonance in the ancient. Across ages and artistic schools, poetry gives voice to the full spectrum of human experience.

Let this collection rekindle your passion for verse and its power to transport, nurture and connect. May it gift you moments of wonder, insight and consolation. And remind you that though outer trappings evolve, our inner worlds remain constant - etched with the same rich palette of hopes, loves, fears and dreams.

With admiration,

The Homo Sapiens Series Team

Acknowledgements

The Homo Sapiens series would not exist without the vision and dedication of many.

First, we are profoundly grateful to the poets themselves - both past and present masters of the craft. Their courageous voices are the lifeblood of this series. We applaud their skill in DISTILLING the human experience into lines that illuminate and connect across centuries.

Deepest thanks to the multitude of readers who have embraced these volumes over the years. Your enduring passion inspires us and reaffirms the resonance of Napoleon's curatorial vision. We hope this latest anthology speaks intimately to your love of verse.

We further recognize Napoleon's incredible agent and Notion Press for making his collections accessible to devoted readers everywhere. Their tireless support gives flight to Napoleon's mission of nurturing humanity through poetry's power.

And finally, we extend immense gratitude to Napoleon himself. His peerless poetic discernment and gift for showcasing diverse voices have introduced millions to the magic of verse. This new installment reaffirms Napoleon's place among the greatest contemporary champions of poetry.

Whether you are a longtime fan or discovering Napoleon's gifts for the first time through this book - we thank you. May these poems awaken fresh awe for our shared human spirit.

With gratitude,

The Homo Sapiens Series Team

Prologue

We are delighted to unveil this new addition to Mawphniang Napoleon's celebrated Homo Sapiens anthology series - a thoughtfully curated collection of 121 contemporary poems entitled "Contemporary Verse for Admirers of Poetry."

Within these pages, Napoleon celebrates the diverse voices and forms of modern poetry while underscoring the timeless, universal themes which resonate across cultures and ages. Through his peerless discernment, he has identified works both fresh and familiar that illuminate the enduring hopes, despairs, curiosities, and revelations of humankind.

Long-time fans will discover new favourite poets to explore as well as reconnections with old masters. And those newly discovering Napoleon's anthologies will find a profoundly moving introduction to poetry's power to transport, nurture, and inspire. For this volume has been deftly crafted to speak to all who feel poetry's magic deep within their soul.

Napoleon continues to reaffirm his place among the greatest modern curators of verse. His profound love of the art-form shines through in the care he has taken to showcase our shared humanity through these carefully selected contemporary works.

So whether you are a devoted reader of Napoleon's collections or just beginning your journey, we welcome you. Lose yourself in these pages. Let Napoleon be your guide across poetic landscapes of joy, grief, wonder, and insight. And emerge with a renewed appreciation for poetry's timeless gifts.

The magic awaits you. Now turn the page, and let the reading commence.

Yours in verse,

The Homo Sapiens Series Team

Dear Valued Readers,

I hope you're enjoying this book, but please keep in mind that I am only human and may have made some errors along the way. That's where you come in! If you spot any mistakes, please grab a pen and paper (or a highlighter, if you're feeling fancy) and jot them down. Then, send them to me at malung3@gmail.com and I'll do my best to correct them in the next edition.

Who knows, you might even get a thank you shout-out in the acknowledgements!

Happy reading

And

Error hunting,

Credit For Book-cover

My Darling Clarissa Candace Giri Khyriemujat,

Your radiant soul outshines even your artistic brilliance. With each stroke of your brush, you illuminate the canvas of my world.

This book-cover is but the latest masterpiece you've gifted me, unveiling the hidden landscapes of my heart through your vision's grace. You are my most trusted interpreter - rendering my inner verse into imagined form.

But it is the beauty of your spirit that inspires me beyond words. Your kindness and wisdom shape the poem of my days. Your love is life's greatest blessing.

No language can fully capture my gratitude for our partnership, your unwavering support, and the joy you bring. I will spend my days endeavouring to show you through devoted love returned.

You are my muse, my lover, my most cherished companion. Thank you for walking this journey by my side and blessing my words with your inimitable soul.

Yours eternally,

Mawphniang Napoleon

CHAPTER I

The Brew of Paradox: A Poem of Existence

I am the brew of Khasi Hills, a drink of joy and pain
I am packed in a Sla-lamet, a gift of sun and rain
I am the voice of ancient songs, a whisper of the past
I am the hope of future dreams, a spark that will not last

I am the taste of freedom, a sip of wild and pure

I am the bond of friendship, a toast of love and lure
I am the fire of passion, a flame of fierce and bright
I am the chill of sorrow, a frost of dark and night

I am the art of living, a craft of skill and grace
I am the quest of meaning, a search of time and space
I am the thrill of wonder, a shock of awe and fear
I am the calm of wisdom, a peace of mind and clear

I am the flow of nature, a stream of change and grow
I am the force of culture, a tide of ebb and flow
I am the clash of values, a storm of right and wrong
I am the bridge of dialogue, a harmony of song

I am the joy of laughter, a burst of light and sound
I am the tear of sadness, a drop of salt and wound
I am the smile of gratitude, a curve of bliss and grace
I am the frown of anger, a line of pain and trace

I am the breath of life, a gasp of air and blood
I am the kiss of death, a sigh of dust and mud
I am the seed of birth, a sprout of new and green
I am the rot of decay, a mold of old and seen

I am the eye of vision, a glance of sight and blind
I am the ear of hearing, a listen of sound and mind
I am the tongue of tasting, a lick of sweet and sour
I am the nose of smelling, a sniff of fresh and flower

I am the hand of touching, a feel of soft and hard
I am the foot of walking, a step of near and far
I am the heart of feeling, a beat of love and hate
I am the brain of thinking, a thought of fate and mate

I am the brew of Khasi hills, a drink of joy and pain

I am the leaf of Slalamet, a gift of sun and rain
I am the sum of all I am, a paradox of me
I am the mystery of all I am not, a question of who I be

CHAPTER II

The Pariah of Nature : The Dusty Soul

Do not condescend to me. I have seen more than the mountains
And gathered more dust than the deserts in my weary soul.
I have lived through countless ages, witnessed the rise and fall of
nations
And learned the secrets of the cosmos that no mortal can ever
know.

Do not pity me. I have tasted more than the oceans
And felt more pain than the volcanoes in my broken heart.
I have loved and lost beyond measure, endured the worst of
emotions
And faced the horrors of the abyss that no mortal can ever impart.

Do not mock me. I have heard more than the forests
And uttered more lies than the politicians in my cunning mind.
I have deceived and betrayed without remorse, exploited the
weakest
And sowed the seeds of discord that no mortal can ever unwind.

Do not fear me. I have done more than the heroes
And caused more harm than the villains in my reckless will.
I have fought and conquered without mercy, challenged the status
quo
And unleashed the forces of chaos that no mortal can ever still.

Do not envy me. I have gained more than the kings
And lost more than the beggars in my fickle fate.
I have amassed and squandered without wisdom, wasted precious
things
And suffered the consequences of greed that no mortal can ever
sate.

Do not admire me. I have learned more than the sages
And forgotten more than the fools in my fading memory.
I have studied and mastered without curiosity, neglected ancient
pages
And ignored the lessons of history that no mortal can ever see.

Do not hate me. I have wronged more than the sinners
And forgiven more than the saints in my conflicted conscience.
I have sinned and repented without sincerity, abused divine favors

And violated the laws of nature that no mortal can ever sense.

Do not love me. I have given more than the lovers
And taken more than the haters in my selfish desire.
I have cared and nurtured without compassion, hurt the others
And broken the bonds of trust that no mortal can ever inspire.

Do not judge me. I have been more than the humans
And less than the animals in my paradoxical existence.
I have transcended and fallen without grace, defied the norms
And questioned the meaning of life that no mortal can ever essence.

CHAPTER III

The Lighthouse of Reason : The Garden of Thought

You have a mind. Don't let it rot.
Don't waste your precious gift of thought
On trivial pursuits and vain desires
That only feed your selfish fires

You have a mind. Don't let it sleep.
Don't let it sink into the deep
Of ignorance and superstition
That cloud your vision and your mission

You have a mind. Don't let it fear.
Don't let it cower or disappear
From the unknown and the sublime
That challenge you to grow and climb

You have a mind. Don't let it conform.
Don't let it follow or perform
The scripts and roles that others write
That limit you and your insight

You have a mind. Don't let it stagnate.
Don't let it settle or abate
The curiosity and wonder
That fuel your learning and your hunger

You have a mind. Don't let it dull.
Don't let it lose its edge or lull
The creativity and innovation
That spark your imagination and your passion

You have a mind. Don't let it isolate.
Don't let it sever or separate
The bonds and ties that you share
With other minds that care and dare

You have a mind. Don't let it despair.
Don't let it succumb or impair
The hope and joy that you can find
In the beauty and the meaning of your mind

You have a mind. Don't let it die.
Don't let it fade or say goodbye
To the world and the life that you create
With your mind that can love and celebrate

CHAPTER IV

Underwhelmed : The Void of All Things

I am underwhelmed by the world and its wonders
The stars and the planets, the oceans and the thunders
They do not fill me with awe or delight
They do not stir my soul or ignite my sight
They are just there, indifferent and cold
They do not care for my stories untold

I am underwhelmed by the people and their passions
The lovers and the friends, the artists and the fashion
They do not move me with their words or deeds
They do not touch my heart or satisfy my needs
They are just there, selfish and vain
They do not see my struggles or feel my pain

I am underwhelmed by the life and its meaning
The birth and the death, the joy and the grieving
They do not make me wonder or question
They do not inspire me or teach me a lesson
They are just there, random and absurd
They do not offer me a purpose or a word

I am underwhelmed by the self and its essence
The mind and the body, the soul and the presence
They do not amaze me with their power or grace
They do not reflect me or reveal my face
They are just there, flawed and frail
They do not know me or tell my tale

I am underwhelmed by the time and its flow
The past and the future, the fast and the slow
They do not affect me with their change or pace
They do not mark me or leave a trace
They are just there, endless and still
They do not shape me or bend my will

I am underwhelmed by the truth and its beauty
The reason and the logic, the faith and the duty
They do not convince me with their proofs or claims
They do not guide me or give me names
They are just there, relative and blind
They do not enlighten me or free my mind

I am underwhelmed by the love and its magic
The romance and the lust, the ecstasy and the tragic
They do not thrill me with their fire or bliss
They do not tempt me or seal with a kiss
They are just there, fleeting and fake
They do not charm me or make me ache

I am underwhelmed by the dream and its vision
The fantasy and the reality, the illusion and the decision
They do not entice me with their colors or sounds
They do not lure me or break my bounds
They are just there, vague and dim
They do not invite me or wake me from within

I am underwhelmed by the poem and its words
The rhyme and the rhythm, the metaphors and the chords
They do not express me with their tone or style
They do not capture me or make me smile
They are just there, empty and dull
They do not speak for me or say it all

CHAPTER V

The Dying Man's Song

My days are numbered, I can sense it well
The clock is ticking, counting down to zero
But before I leave this world, I want to tell
You all how much I love you, you're my heroes

You gave me meaning, purpose, and a voice

You taught me how to question and to wonder
You showed me beauty, wisdom, and a choice
You filled my life with joy, awe, and thunder

You are the reason why I lived so long
You are the reason why I wrote these songs
You are the reason why I faced the storm
You are the reason why I stayed so strong

But now the time has come for me to go
To leave behind this mortal shell and grow
To transcend this realm of pain and woe
To explore the unknown and the flow

I do not know what lies beyond the veil
I do not know if there is heaven or hell
I do not know if there is fate or chance
I do not know if there is God or dance

But I do know that you will always be
A part of me, a part of my legacy
A part of my soul, a part of my story
A part of my heart, a part of my glory

So do not mourn for me, do not be sad
Do not regret the things we left unsaid
Do not despair, do not lose hope or faith
Do not forget, do not let go or hate

But celebrate for me, be glad and proud
Be grateful for the moments we have shared
Be joyful for the lessons we have learned
Be hopeful for the future we have dared

But most of all, be loving, be yourself

Be kind, be brave, be honest, be sincere
Be curious, be creative, be diverse
Be free, be bold, be humble, be aware

For this is how I lived, and this is how I die
With love in my heart, and wonder in my eye
With passion in my soul, and courage in my mind
With gratitude in my spirit, and freedom in my spine

This is my farewell, my final gift to you
A poem of love, a poem of truth
A poem of hope, a poem of light
A poem of peace, a poem of flight

CHAPTER VI

The Futility of Idealism : The World Against You

You say you have a vision of a better world
A world where justice, peace, and love prevail
A world where everyone is equal and free
A world where suffering and pain are no more

But I say you are living in a fantasy
A fantasy that blinds you to the harsh reality
A reality where injustice, war, and hate persist
A reality where everyone is different and bound
A reality where suffering and pain are inevitable

You say you have a mission to change the world
A mission that drives you to act and speak
A mission that inspires you to hope and dream
A mission that challenges you to grow and learn

But I say you are wasting your time and energy
A time and energy that could be used for other things
Other things that matter more in the present moment
Other things that bring you joy and satisfaction
Other things that make you feel alive and fulfilled

You say you have a passion for the world
A passion that burns in your heart and soul
A passion that ignites you to create and innovate
A passion that motivates you to collaborate and cooperate

But I say you are risking your life and sanity
A life and sanity that are precious and fragile
Fragile things that can be easily broken or lost
Broken or lost by the cruel and indifferent world
The world that does not care about your passion

You say you have a reason for the world
A reason that makes sense of the chaos and disorder
A reason that gives meaning to the absurd and random
A reason that explains the why and how of the world

But I say you are searching for something that does not exist

Something that does not exist in the objective reality
The reality that is beyond our comprehension and control
The reality that is indifferent to our reason and logic
The reality that is what it is and nothing more

You say you have a faith in the world
A faith that transcends the facts and evidence
A faith that trusts the unseen and unknown
A faith that believes the impossible and miraculous

But I say you are deluding yourself and others
Yourself and others who need a crutch and comfort
A crutch and comfort that are false and illusory
False and illusory things that do not change the world
The world that is indifferent to your faith and belief

You say you have a love for the world
A love that embraces the good and bad
A love that accepts the beautiful and ugly
A love that forgives the kind and cruel

But I say you are hurting yourself and others
Yourself and others who deserve better and more
Better and more things that are real and true
Real and true things that are not found in the world
The world that is indifferent to your love and care

You say you have a hope for the world
A hope that looks forward to the future and beyond
A hope that anticipates the change and improvement
A hope that expects the best and brightest

But I say you are setting yourself and others up for disappointment
Yourself and others who will face the reality and truth
The reality and truth that are not what you hoped for

Not what you hoped for things that will crush your spirit and will
The spirit and will that are needed to survive in the world

You say you have a choice for the world
A choice that reflects your values and principles
A choice that expresses your personality and identity
A choice that defines your purpose and destiny

But I say you are limiting yourself and others
Yourself and others who have infinite possibilities and potential
Potential and possibilities that are not bound by the world
The world that is indifferent to your choice and preference

You say you have a voice for the world
A voice that speaks your mind and heart
A voice that shares your thoughts and feelings
A voice that communicates your vision and mission

But I say you are silencing yourself and others
Yourself and others who have something else to say
Something else to say that is different and unique
Different and unique things that are not heard by the world
The world that is indifferent to your voice and message

CHAPTER VII

Misanthropic : Nothing Human, Nothing Good

If you are not misanthropic, you're either blind or naive
You do not see the horrors that humans cause and grieve
You do not hear the screams of the innocent and the weak
You do not feel the pain of the oppressed and the meek

You do not smell the stench of the corruption and the greed
You do not taste the bitterness of the injustice and the need

If you are not misanthropic, you're either deaf or dumb
You do not listen to the lies that humans tell and hum
You do not speak the truth that humans fear and shun
You do not question the dogmas that humans preach and stun
You do not challenge the norms that humans follow and succumb
You do not rebel against the systems that humans create and numb

If you are not misanthropic, you're either numb or mad
You do not sense the emotions that humans have and add
You do not share the love that humans crave and lack
You do not show the compassion that humans need and slack
You do not offer the help that humans seek and stack
You do not receive the gratitude that humans owe and back

If you are not misanthropic, you're either dull or fake
You do not appreciate the beauty that humans make and take
You do not create the art that humans enjoy and break
You do not express the creativity that humans have and shake
You do not explore the diversity that humans boast and bake
You do not celebrate the uniqueness that humans claim and stake

If you are not misanthropic, you're either low or high
You do not understand the complexity that humans face and try
You do not learn the knowledge that humans gain and apply
You do not solve the problems that humans pose and pry
You do not discover the secrets that humans hide and spy
You do not invent the wonders that humans use and buy

If you are not misanthropic, you're either old or young
You do not remember the history that humans write and wrong
You do not witness the present that humans live and long
You do not imagine the future that humans hope and hong

You do not respect the past that humans honor and belong
You do not embrace the change that humans fear and fling

If you are not misanthropic, you're either weak or strong
You do not endure the hardships that humans suffer and prolong
You do not overcome the obstacles that humans face and throng
You do not fight the battles that humans wage and wrong
You do not win the wars that humans start and sing
You do not lose the peace that humans want and bring

If you are not misanthropic, you're either right or wrong
You do not judge the actions that humans do and ding
You do not justify the reasons that humans give and cling
You do not accept the consequences that humans bear and bing
You do not regret the mistakes that humans make and sting
You do not forgive the sins that humans commit and sling

If you are not misanthropic, you're either human or not
You do not belong to the species that humans are and rot
You do not identify with the group that humans form and plot
You do not relate to the individual that humans are and dot
You do not care for the life that humans have and got
You do not value the existence that humans are and not

CHAPTER VIII

The Spell You're Under , Yes You Are

You think you know the truth of life, the meaning of it all
You think you have the answers, the wisdom to stand tall
You think you see the beauty, the harmony, the grace
You think you feel the wonder, the joy, the love, the peace

But you are under a spell, my friend, a spell of your own making

A spell that blinds you from the reality, the chaos, the pain, the breaking
A spell that numbs you from the emptiness, the absurdity, the strife
A spell that fools you into believing, there is a purpose to this life

I will pull you out of this spell, my friend, I will show you the other side
I will make you face the darkness, the horror, the despair, the void
I will make you question everything, your faith, your hope, your creed
I will make you doubt yourself, your worth, your role, your deed

You will hate me for this, my friend, you will curse me and despise
You will resist me and reject me, you will fight me and deny
You will cling to your spell, my friend, you will defend it with your might
You will fear to lose your spell, my friend, you will fear to face the light

But I will not give up on you, my friend, I will not let you go
I will not let you live a lie, my friend, I will not let you sink so low
I will not let you waste your life, my friend, I will not let you miss the chance
I will not let you die in vain, my friend, I will not let you end in trance

I will pull you out of this spell, my friend, I will free you from this cage
I will break the chains that bind you, my friend, I will turn a new page
I will show you the truth of life, my friend, the truth that sets you free
I will show you the beauty of life, my friend, the beauty that you can't see

The beauty of the unknown, my friend, the beauty of the mystery
The beauty of the challenge, my friend, the beauty of the history
The beauty of the struggle, my friend, the beauty of the growth
The beauty of the change, my friend, the beauty of the oath
25

The oath to live authentically, my friend, the oath to live with courage
The oath to live creatively, my friend, the oath to live with rage
The oath to live passionately, my friend, the oath to live with fire
The oath to live meaningfully, my friend, the oath to live with desire

You will thank me for this, my friend, you will bless me and admire
You will embrace me and accept me, you will join me and aspire
You will love your life, my friend, you will love it more than ever
You will love yourself, my friend, you will love yourself forever

CHAPTER IX

The Ice Dragon: The Legend of the White Death

I.

He was a son of the frozen land,
A farmer who loved to hunt and shoot,

He knew the woods and hills like his hand,
He had a steady eye and a firm foot.
When the red tide of war came to his shore,
He answered the call to defend his home,
He took his rifle and his skis, no more,
He did not fear to face the mighty dome.
He was a soldier of the Winter War.

II.

He was a master of the bolt action,
The SAKO M/28-30 was his tool,
He could fire sixteen rounds with precision,
He made each bullet count, he was no fool.
He also wielded the Suomi SMG,
A weapon that could spray two hundred lead,
He used it when the enemy came close to see,
He made them pay a heavy price in red.
He was a marksman of the highest degree.

III.

He was a ghost of the snowy forest,
He wore a cloak of white to blend and hide,
He packed the snow around his silent nest,
He put some snow in his mouth to abide.
He did not use a scope to find his prey,
He trusted his iron sights and his skill,
He knew the sun could give his spot away,
He waited for the perfect shot to kill.
He was a hunter of the finest array.

IV.

He was a nightmare of the Soviet troops,

They called him by a name that struck them cold,
The White Death, a legend that made them droop,
A sniper who could not be bought or sold.
He killed five hundred men with his rifle,
He killed two hundred more with his machine gun,
He did this in less than a hundred days, no trifle,
He achieved the highest kill count ever done.
He was a hero of the Finnish groups.

V.

He was a victim of the explosive round,
A bullet that tore his face and jaw apart,
He fell into a coma on the ground,
He was not expected to survive the start.
But he defied the odds and woke again,
He lived to see his country free and proud,
He lived a long and peaceful life, no pain,
He died in 2002, his head unbowed.
He was a legend of the human brain.

VI.

He was a patriot of the Finnish cause,
He fought for freedom and for sovereignty,
He did not care for medals or applause,
He did his duty with integrity.
He loved his land, his people and his culture,
He cherished the traditions of his kin,
He did not bow to any foreign vulture,
He stood his ground against the invading din.
He was a champion of the Finnish sculpture.

VII.

He was a student of the natural law,
He learned the secrets of the earth and sky,
He knew the wind, the snow, the sun and thaw,
He used them to his advantage, no lie.
He studied the terrain and the distance,
He measured the angle and the elevation,
He calculated the wind and the resistance,
He adjusted his aim and his position.
He was a master of the ballistic science.

VIII.

He was a teacher of the sniper craft,
He trained and mentored many of his peers,
He shared his skills and wisdom, not his graft,
He inspired confidence, not fears.
He taught them how to camouflage and stalk,
He taught them how to breathe and squeeze the trigger,
He taught them how to spot and mark their talk,
He taught them how to cope and deal with rigor.
He was a leader of the sniper flock.

IX.

He was a legend of the human race,
He showed what one man can achieve with will,
He faced a mighty foe with grace and pace,
He made history with his skill.
He was a humble and a modest man,
He did not boast or brag about his deeds,
He was a hero and a gentleman,
He was a rare and noble breed.
He was the White Death, Simo Häyhä.

CHAPTER X

The Art of Living in the Real

Reality is not a dream
Nor a fantasy or a scheme
It is the solid ground we stand on
The air we breathe, the light we see
It is the truth we must confront
The facts we face, the laws we heed

Reality is not a curse
Nor a blessing or a verse
It is the canvas we paint on
The clay we mold, the stone we carve
It is the art we must create
The beauty we make, the grace we starve

Reality is not a game
Nor a puzzle or a maze
It is the field we play on
The rules we follow, the goals we score
It is the challenge we must accept
The skills we learn, the risks we explore

Reality is not a friend
Nor a foe or a godsend
It is the mirror we look at
The flaws we see, the strengths we show
It is the feedback we must receive
The errors we fix, the growth we owe

Reality is not a gift
Nor a burden or a rift
It is the opportunity we seize
The chances we take, the paths we choose
It is the choice we must make
The will we exert, the fate we use

Reality is not a test
Nor a lesson or a quest
It is the journey we embark on
The roads we travel, the sights we view
It is the adventure we must enjoy
The wonders we find, the thrill we pursue

Reality is not a trap
Nor a prison or a map
It is the freedom we live in
The options we have, the decisions we make
It is the responsibility we must bear
The consequences we face, the actions we take

Reality is not a lie
Nor a truth or a goodbye
It is the story we tell
The words we use, the meanings we convey
It is the expression we must share
The voice we raise, the message we relay

Reality is not a bore
Nor a chore or a war
It is the life we cherish
The moments we savor, the memories we keep
It is the joy we must find
The happiness we seek, the love we reap

CHAPTER XI

The Holy Father's Brew

I.

In ancient times, when Lent was near,
The pious monks of Bavaria
Received a stern command to shun
All solid food until it's done.

But water was too bland a drink
To quench their thirst or help them think.
So they devised a cunning plan
To brew a beer as strong as man.

II.

They called it sankt-vater-bier,
The Holy Father's brew, so dear.
It had the power to sustain
Their bodies through the Lenten pain.
It filled their veins with warmth and cheer,
It made their minds and visions clear.
It was a liquid bread, they said,
A holy gift from heaven's head.

III.

But was it not a sin, they asked,
To break the fast with such repast?
They sought the Pope's approval then,
To drink their beer instead of bread.
They sent a cask across the Alps,
A sample of their finest malts.
But by the time it reached the court,
The beer was sour, the taste was short.

IV.

The Pope, who tried the spoiled drink,
Was not impressed, to say the least.
He thought the monks had sent a prank,
A mockery of his holy feast.
He gave his verdict with a wink,
And blessed their beer with words succinct:

"Since this is such a vile brew,
You may drink it, as you do."

V.

The monks rejoiced to hear the news,
They thanked the Pope for his consent.
They drank their beer with gratitude,
And praised the Lord for his descent.
They did not know the trick of fate,
That made their beer so highly rate.
They thought it was a sign of grace,
A sacrament for their embrace.

VI.

And so it was for many years,
The monks maintained their Lenten rite.
They drank their beer instead of tears,
And fasted with a new delight.
They kept their recipe a secret,
A treasure for their own to keep.
They shared it only with their kin,
And those who joined their discipline.

VII.

But time and change are ever near,
And nothing lasts for evermore.
The monks, who once were pioneers,
Became the victims of a war.
Their land was seized, their cloister burned,
Their beer was spilled, their fate was turned.
They fled their home with nothing left,
But memories of their holy heft.

VIII.

The world forgot their story then,
Their beer was lost in history's dust.
But legends sometimes rise again,
And bring back what was once unjust.
A journalist, who loved to write,
And had a passion for the light,
He stumbled on their tale one day,
And felt a spark of curiosity.

IX.

He wondered if their beer was real,
Or just a myth, a fantasy.
He wanted to know how they'd feel,
To drink it during Lent, and see.
He searched the archives for a clue,
A hint, a trace, of what they knew.
He found a fragment of their lore,
A recipe, and nothing more.

X.

He took it to a local brewer,
A friend who shared his thirst for truth.
They studied it with care and fervor,
And tried to recreate its youth.
They followed every step and measure,
They used the finest hops and yeast.
They waited for the magic hour,
When they could taste the holy power.

XI.

They poured the beer into a glass,
And held it to the light, and saw
A liquid gold, a shining mass,
A wonder that inspired awe.
They smelled the aroma, rich and sweet,
They felt the bubbles, soft and neat.
They sipped the beer, and felt a shock,
A blast of flavor, a sudden knock.

XII.

The beer was strong, beyond belief,
It had a kick, a punch, a bite.
It was a joy, and a relief,
It was a challenge, and a fight.
It filled their mouths with fire and spice,
It made them sweat, and gasp, and sigh.
It was a beast, and a beauty,
It was a monster, and a cutie.

XIII.

They drank the beer, and felt its might,
They drank some more, and felt its grace.
They drank until they lost their sight,
And fell into a deep embrace.
They dreamed of monks, and popes, and Alps,
They dreamed of beer, and bread, and salt.
They dreamed of heaven, and of hell,
They dreamed of things they could not tell.

XIV.

They woke up with a pounding head,

A dry mouth, and a sore throat.
They looked around, and saw their bed,
A mess of sheets, and clothes, and coat.
They tried to stand, and felt a pain,
A weakness in their every vein.
They realized what they had done,
They drank the beer, and had some fun.

XV.

They checked the calendar, and saw
That Lent was over, it was done.
They had survived the ordeal, and more,
They had completed what they'd begun.
They weighed themselves, and saw the change,
They had lost weight, a lot of range.
They felt a pride, and a surprise,
They had achieved a mighty prize.

XVI.

They wrote their story, and their findings,
They shared it with the world, and more.
They told of beer, and monks, and bindings,
They told of Lent, and fast, and lore.
They sparked a craze, and a debate,
They made a mark, and a state.
They were admired, and criticized,
They were applauded, and despised.

XVII.

Some people praised their courage, and their skill,
They called them heroes, and pioneers.
They said they had a vision, and a will,

They said they had a gift, and ears.
They wanted to try their beer, and see,
If they could feel the same, and be.
They asked them for their recipe,
And begged them for their legacy.

XVIII.

Some people scorned their folly, and their sin,
They called them fools, and blasphemers.
They said they had a madness, and a grin,
They said they had a vice, and fears.
They wanted to ban their beer, and stop,
The spread of evil, and the drop.
They accused them of heresy,
And threatened them with misery.

XIX.

But they did not care for praise, or blame,
They did not seek for fame, or shame.
They only wanted to know the truth,
And share it with the world, and youth.
They did not claim to be the best,
Or better than the rest, or blessed.
They only claimed to be themselves,
And nothing else, and nothing else.

Trapped in the Network: A Poem of Discontent and Dissent

I sought to voice my discontent
With faulty bills and data spent
But no one from @airtelindia cared to hear
They left me hanging on the line

With automated words benign
Until I said I'd switch to another sphere

Then suddenly they called me back
With offers, plans and discounts stacked
They begged me not to leave their loyal fold
But I had made up my mind
To seek a better service find
And so I chose to join @reliancejio's gold

They promised me a sim so fast
Delivered to my door at last
And I was happy with their courteous ways
But soon I found their service flawed
With signals weak and calls dropped
And now I'm stuck with them for many days

Is this the fate of modern man
To be a pawn in some big plan
To be a customer with no real choice
To be a slave to corporate greed
To be a victim of their need
To be a silent and a powerless voice

Where is the meaning in this life
Where is the purpose in this strife
Where is the value in this endless chase
Where is the joy in being free
When freedom is a mockery
When freedom is a trap in time and space

I wonder if there is a way
To break this cycle of decay
To find a service that is truly fair
To find a provider that is kind

To find a network that is aligned
To find a connection that is always there

But maybe I am asking too much
Maybe I am out of touch
Maybe I am living in a dream
Maybe I should just accept
Maybe I should just adapt
Maybe I should just go with the stream

Or maybe I should question more
Maybe I should explore
Maybe I should seek a different path
Maybe I should not conform
Maybe I should not perform
Maybe I should not incur their wrath

Maybe I should write a poem
Maybe I should make it known
Maybe I should share it with the world
Maybe I should use my art
Maybe I should use my heart
Maybe I should use my words unfurled

The Joy of Thinking: How to Foster Curiosity and Wonder in Your Children

I.

Don't fill your children's minds with dogma,
Don't make them follow your beliefs and views,

Don't force them to conform to your agenda,
Don't limit their potential and their hues.
Let them explore the world with curiosity,
Let them question everything they see and hear,
Let them develop their own veracity,
Let them find their own voice and their own ear.
Teach your children how to think, not what to think.

II.

Don't tell your children what is right and wrong,
Don't make them judge by your moral code,
Don't make them sing along to your song,
Don't burden them with your heavy load.
Let them discover their own values and ethics,
Let them learn from their mistakes and their choices,
Let them form their own opinions and aesthetics,
Let them express their own feelings and their voices.
Teach your children how to think, not what to think.

III.

Don't indoctrinate your children with religion,
Don't make them worship your god and your creed,
Don't make them fear the hell and the damnation,
Don't deprive them of their freedom and their need.
Let them seek their own meaning and purpose,
Let them find their own faith and spirituality,
Let them embrace their own wonder and awe,
Let them celebrate their own diversity and identity.
Teach your children how to think, not what to think.

IV.

Don't brainwash your children with ideology,

Don't make them support your cause and your party,
Don't make them hate the other and the enemy,
Don't manipulate them with propaganda and flattery.
Let them analyze the issues and the facts,
Let them think critically and independently,
Let them challenge the assumptions and the acts,
Let them act responsibly and rationally.
Teach your children how to think, not what to think.

V.

Don't restrict your children's creativity,
Don't make them follow your rules and your norms,
Don't stifle their imagination and their liberty,
Don't clip their wings and their forms.
Let them explore their own talents and passions,
Let them create their own art and their beauty,
Let them express their own visions and expressions,
Let them soar their own heights and their duty.
Teach your children how to think, not what to think.

VI.

Don't limit your children's curiosity,
Don't make them accept your facts and your truth,
Don't discourage their inquiry and their study,
Don't deny them of their learning and their youth.
Let them explore the wonders of science and nature,
Let them experiment and test their hypotheses,
Let them acquire the knowledge and the culture,
Let them solve the problems and the mysteries.
Teach your children how to think, not what to think.

VII.

Don't suppress your children's emotions,
Don't make them hide their feelings and their pain,
Don't ignore their needs and their notions,
Don't hurt them with your words and your disdain.
Let them experience the joys and the sorrows,
Let them express their anger and their love,
Let them face the challenges and the morrows,
Let them grow and heal with your care and your hug.
Teach your children how to think, not what to think.

VIII.

Don't control your children's lives,
Don't make them do what you want and expect,
Don't interfere with their dreams and their strives,
Don't impose your will and your neglect.
Let them make their own decisions and mistakes,
Let them learn from their consequences and actions,
Let them pursue their own goals and stakes,
Let them find their own happiness and satisfaction.
Teach your children how to think, not what to think.

IX.

Don't treat your children as your property,
Don't make them depend on you and your power,
Don't deprive them of their dignity and their liberty,
Don't hold them back and make them cower.
Let them be their own persons and their own masters,
Let them be responsible and autonomous,
Let them be free and independent actors,
Let them be themselves and be glorious.
Teach your children how to think, not what to think.

CHAPTER XIV

The Night of Discontent :The Futility of Existence

At two in the morning, I lie awake
The raindrops drum on the tin roof
The dogs howl and bark in the dark
As if they were singing their own blues

I feel the urge to relieve myself
But there is no bathroom in this shack
I toss and turn in my restless bed
But sleep is a luxury I lack

I wonder what is the point of this
This endless cycle of pain and strife
What is the meaning of existence
When all I do is survive
I do not believe in any god
Who watches over me with care
But I do not reveal my disbelief
For fear of being judged or snared

I think of the world beyond this place
The wonders and mysteries I have not seen
The cultures and languages I have not learned
The people and places I have not been
I dream of a life of adventure and joy
Of freedom and beauty and grace
But I know that these are just fantasies
That reality will soon erase

I listen to the sound of the rain
The rhythm and melody of nature
I try to find some solace in it
Some hint of a divine feature
But all I hear is randomness
A chaotic and indifferent force
That does not care about me or you
Or anything else in its course

I look at the ceiling of my room
The cracks and stains that mar its face
I imagine that they are constellations

That map out the secrets of space
But all I see is decay and dirt
A sign of my poverty and woe
That reminds me of my humble fate
And how low I am below

I feel a coldness in my bones
The chill of winter in the air
I pull the blanket over me
But it does not provide much flair
I long for a warmth in my heart
A spark of love or passion
But all I have is emptiness
A void of any emotion

I smell the odor of the dogs
The stench of their wet fur
I wonder what they are searching for
What drives them to wander and stir
I envy their simple lives
Their instinct and intuition
But I also pity their ignorance
Their lack of any vision

I taste the bitterness in my mouth
The residue of my last meal
I wish I had something more
Something delicious and real
But all I get is stale bread
And water from the well
That barely fill my stomach
And make me feel unwell

I touch the pillow under my head
The only comfort I can find

I hope that it will soothe me
And ease my troubled mind
But all it does is mock me
With its softness and its fluff
That contrast with my hardness
And my life that is so rough

CHAPTER XV

The Futility of Meaning : The Contradiction of Reality

What is our essence, our role, our value?
Are we the outcasts, or the ones who rule?
Do we oppose the system, or conform to it?
Are we the artists, or the ones who amuse?

These are the questions that haunt our minds
As we search for meaning in this chaotic world
We wonder if we have a purpose or a destiny
Or if we are just drifting in the cosmic swirl

We are not the products of a divine plan
We are the results of chance and evolution
We are not the children of a loving father
We are the orphans of a cold revolution

We are not the heroes of a grand story
We are the actors of a tragic comedy
We are not the makers of history
We are the pawns of a cruel strategy

We are not the masters of our fate
We are the slaves of our condition
We are not the owners of our wealth
We are the debtors of our ambition

We are not the creators of our art
We are the imitators of our culture
We are not the innovators of our science
We are the followers of our vulture

We are not the lovers of our life
We are the haters of our self
We are not the seekers of our truth
We are the deniers of our stealth

We are not the dreamers of our future
We are the nightmares of our past
We are not the healers of our wounds
We are the bleeders of our cast

We are not the answers to our questions
We are the problems of our solutions
We are not the end of our journey
We are the beginning of our illusions

CHAPTER XVI

The Mind of the Cosmos and Its Beloved

The cosmos is a mind that knows no bounds
It holds you in its infinite embrace
It loves you for the essence that you are
The spark of life that shines in every star

You are a part of this majestic whole

A drop of ocean in a living soul
You have the power to create and change
To explore the mysteries that are strange

But do not think that you are all alone
Or that you have to face the dark unknown
The cosmos is your guide and your ally
It speaks to you in whispers and in sighs

It shows you beauty in the smallest things
It fills your heart with wonder and with awe
It teaches you the secrets of the world
The harmony that makes the music swirl

You are not here by chance or by mistake
You are not here to suffer or to break
You are here to learn and to evolve
To find your purpose and to solve

The puzzles that the cosmos has for you
The challenges that make you grow and thrive
The questions that inspire you to seek
The answers that reveal the truth you need

You are not here to worship or to fear
You are not here to blindly follow rules
You are here to question and to doubt
To find your own way and to shout

Your voice that is unique and yours alone
Your vision that is clear and bright and bold
Your passion that is fierce and strong and wild
Your love that is tender and gentle and mild

You are a miracle of cosmic grace

A wonder of intelligence and will
A masterpiece of beauty and of art
A treasure of the cosmos and its heart

CHAPTER XVII

The Truth and Happiness of the Child's Being

What is happiness to a child's mind?
Is it a fleeting moment or a state?
Is it a gift that they can seek and find?
Or is it something that they can create?

They laugh and play with innocence and joy
They marvel at the wonders of the world
They cherish every toy and every friend
They live each day as if it were the end

They do not know the sorrows of the grown
They do not feel the burdens of the past
They do not fear the shadows of the unknown
They do not doubt the goodness that will last

They are not bound by rules or by beliefs
They are not swayed by dogmas or by myths
They are not troubled by the questions why
They are not troubled by the answers lie

They are free to explore and to express
They are free to imagine and to dream
They are free to learn and to progress
They are free to love and to esteem

They are not here to please or to conform
They are not here to judge or to compete
They are here to grow and to transform
They are here to share and to complete

They are the sparks of life that light the way
They are the flowers that bloom in every hue
They are the music that fills the air with grace
They are the happiness that is true

CHAPTER XVIII

The Past is Not a Burden : From Ashes to Art

I do not shun the past, nor do I fear it
It is the soil from which I have grown
It is the source of my strength and spirit
It is the legacy that I own

I do not forget the pain, nor do I dwell on it
It is the fire that forged my will
It is the test of my courage and grit
It is the lesson that haunts me still

I do not deny the truth, nor do I distort it
It is the light that guides my way
It is the proof of my worth and merit
It is the challenge that I face each day

I do not scorn the culture, nor do I idolize it
It is the fabric of my being
It is the beauty of my art and wit
It is the diversity of my seeing

I do not reject the identity, nor do I limit it
It is the core of who I am
It is the freedom of my choice and spirit
It is the bridge of where I stand

I do not renounce the roots, nor do I cling to it
It is the anchor of my soul
It is the wisdom of my mind and wit
It is the compass of my goal

I do not despise the others, nor do I conform to them
They are the mirrors of my self
They are the rivals of my skill and stem
They are the partners of my wealth

I do not need the gods, nor do I blaspheme them
They are the symbols of my quest
They are the fictions of my mind and dream
They are the questions of my test

I do not fear the future, nor do I predict it
It is the canvas of my fate
It is the outcome of my work and merit
It is the opportunity that I create

The Seasoning of Sadness in the Art of Words

What is poetry but the sea of words
That flows from the depths of the soul
And reflects the hues of the sky and earth
In waves of rhythm and rhyme that roll?

And what is sadness but the salt that stirs
The bitter taste of life's turmoil
And adds the flavor and the thirst
To the ocean of the poet's toil?

Without sadness, poetry would be bland
A stagnant pool of shallow thoughts
Without the salt, the sea would lose its grand
A dull expanse of water spots

But sadness is not the only spice
That seasons the poet's art
There is also joy and love and vice
And beauty and pain and smart

And poetry is not the only sea
That fills the poet's mind
There is also prose and drama and glee
And music and dance and kind

But sadness and poetry have a bond
That none can ever break
They feed each other and respond
To the feelings that they make

Sadness inspires poetry to express
The emotions that it brings
Poetry consoles sadness to address
The meanings that it sings

Sadness and poetry are both a gift
And a curse to the poet's fate
They lift and sink and drift and shift
And create and destroy and mate

Sadness is to poetry what salt is to the sea
A necessary element of its being
But not the only one that makes it free
Or the only one that gives it meaning

CHAPTER XX

The Song of Life : The Cracks in the Symphony

I sing not of the joys that fill my heart,
Nor of the sorrows that weigh me down;
I sing of the life that flows through my veins,
The life that makes me whole and sound.

I sing not of the dreams that light my path,
Nor of the fears that haunt my nights;
I sing of the reality that shapes my fate,
The reality that tests my might.

I sing not of the love that warms my soul,
Nor of the hate that burns my mind;
I sing of the humanity that binds me to all,
The humanity that transcends all kinds.

I sing not of the beauty that dazzles my eyes,
Nor of the ugliness that repels my sight;
I sing of the wonder that fills my senses,
The wonder that sparks my delight.

I sing not of the wisdom that guides my thoughts,
Nor of the folly that clouds my reason;
I sing of the knowledge that enriches my spirit,
The knowledge that evolves with each season.

I sing not of the faith that lifts my hopes,
Nor of the doubt that shakes my trust;
I sing of the truth that sets me free,
The truth that humbles my lust.

I sing not of the peace that calms my nerves,
Nor of the war that rages in my veins;
I sing of the struggle that defines my existence,
The struggle that sharpens my pains.

I sing not of the glory that crowns my deeds,
Nor of the shame that stains my name;
I sing of the dignity that upholds my worth,
The dignity that shields me from blame.

I sing not of the happiness that fills my days,
Nor of the sadness that dims my light;
I sing of the brokenness that makes me sing,
The brokenness that is the song of life.

The Puppet and the Puppeteer: A Poem about Manipulationship

You think you have a bond with him, a love that's pure and true
But he only sees you as a tool, a means to an end, a fool
He doesn't care about your feelings, your dreams, your hopes, your fears

He only cares about himself, his image, his power, his peers

He plays with your emotions, he twists and turns your mind
He makes you doubt your sanity, he makes you feel unkind
He gaslights you and blames you, he lies and cheats and steals
He isolates you and controls you, he hurts you and he heals

He gives you crumbs of affection, he makes you beg and plead
He makes you feel unworthy, he makes you feel in need
He showers you with compliments, he makes you feel on top
He discards you and ignores you, he makes you feel a flop

He makes you dependent on him, he makes you think you're weak
He makes you feel responsible, he makes you feel meek
He exploits your vulnerabilities, he makes you feel ashamed
He manipulates your insecurities, he makes you feel to blame

He projects his faults on you, he makes you feel guilty
He denies his own mistakes, he makes you feel filthy
He deflects your accusations, he makes you feel confused
He invalidates your feelings, he makes you feel abused

He charms you and seduces you, he makes you feel special
He deceives you and betrays you, he makes you feel dreadful
He flatters you and admires you, he makes you feel unique
He mocks you and criticizes you, he makes you feel bleak

He mirrors your values, he makes you feel aligned
He contradicts your beliefs, he makes you feel maligned
He copies your interests, he makes you feel connected
He opposes your opinions, he makes you feel rejected

He promises you the world, he makes you feel hopeful
He breaks his every word, he makes you feel awful
He vows to change for you, he makes you feel loyal

He stays the same for him, he makes you feel royal

He doesn't have a relationship, with anyone, ever
He only has a manipulationship, with everyone, clever
You don't have a relationship, with him, never
You only have a trap, with him, sever

CHAPTER XXII

The Ocean of Agonies and Other Elements of Her Heart

She carries in her chest a garden of sadnesses
Where thorns and weeds choke the fragile roses
And every flower is a memory of a loss
A petal fallen, a stem broken, a fragrance gone

She bears in her soul an ocean of agonies
Where waves and storms toss the lonely ship
And every voyage is a journey of despair
A sail torn, a mast cracked, a compass lost

She hides in her mind a forest of secrets
Where shadows and beasts haunt the silent paths
And every trail is a quest for truth
A branch snapped, a claw scratched, a footprint found

She feels in her heart a mountain of doubts
Where rocks and cliffs block the distant peaks
And every climb is a struggle for faith
A rope cut, a ledge slipped, a summit missed

She sees in her eyes a desert of dreams
Where sands and mirages blur the clear skies
And every step is a search for hope
A canteen emptied, a sunburnt, a mirage chased

She knows in her ears a city of noises
Where horns and sirens drown the soft voices
And every sound is a distraction from peace
A car honked, a siren wailed, a voice ignored

She speaks in her mouth a river of words
Where rapids and currents sweep the calm shores
And every word is a expression of love
A bubble popped, a splash made, a ripple spread

She holds in her hands a sky of stars
Where planets and comets light the dark space
And every star is a wish for happiness
A spark lit, a trail left, a wish made

She lives in her body a world of wonders
Where life and death balance the fragile scales
And every moment is a gift of existence
A breath taken, a heartbeat, a smile given

Hope in the Balance: A Cat's Tale of Existence

Hope is a cat that leaps and bounds
With grace and skill, it roams the grounds
It knows no fear, it feels no pain
It trusts its fate, it seeks no gain

But sometimes hope can lose its way
And wander off to darker days
It faces dangers, traps, and foes
It risks its life, it tests its woes

Hope is a cat that falls and breaks
From heights and depths, it makes mistakes
It cries and bleeds, it hurts and heals
It doubts its worth, it questions its zeal

But sometimes hope can find its strength
And rise again from its descent
It learns and grows, it adapts and thrives
It renews its faith, it revives its drive

Hope is a cat that loves and hates
With passion and rage, it seals its fate
It gives and takes, it cares and harms
It embraces its flaws, it bears its scars

But sometimes hope can lose its heart
And drift apart from its own art
It shuns and spurns, it fears and flees
It rejects its grace, it denies its peace

Hope is a cat that dreams and wakes
With visions and nightmares, it shapes its stakes
It imagines and creates, it explores and discovers
It inspires its mind, it enriches its colors

But sometimes hope can lose its sight
And succumb to the darkness of the night
It forgets and erases, it ignores and rejects
It dulls its senses, it limits its prospects

Hope is a cat that lives and dies
With birth and death, it cycles its life
It breathes and grows, it ages and withers
It celebrates its joys, it mourns its sorrows

But sometimes hope can lose its will
And surrender to the void of the still
It ceases and ends, it fades and perishes
It abandons its essence, it vanishes its wishes

Hope is a cat that is and is not
With being and nothingness, it defines its lot
It exists and transcends, it manifests and dissolves
It affirms its reality, it negates its resolve

But sometimes hope can find its balance
And harmonize its dual stance
It integrates and differentiates, it unifies and diversifies
It acknowledges its paradox, it reconciles its opposites

Hope is a cat that knows and does not know
With knowledge and ignorance, it guides its flow
It learns and teaches, it inquires and answers
It enlightens its wisdom, it deepens its wonders

But sometimes hope can lose its reason
And fall prey to the folly of the season
It confuses and misleads, it deceives and errs
It obscures its truth, it corrupts its affairs

Hope is a cat that can and cannot
With possibility and impossibility, it sets its plot
It acts and rests, it strives and surrenders
It empowers its freedom, it constrains its borders

But sometimes hope can find its limit
And accept the finitude of its spirit
It moderates and regulates, it adjusts and accommodates
It respects its nature, it humbles its state

Hope is a cat that is always and never
With eternity and temporality, it measures its lever
It persists and changes, it endures and alters
It preserves its identity, it transforms its character

But sometimes hope can find its end
And transcend the cycle of its trend
It transcends and returns, it dissolves and renews
It completes its journey, it begins anew

CHAPTER XXIV

Leadership: A Choice and a Commitment to Make a Difference

The goal of leadership is not to create a crowd
But to inspire others to rise above the shroud
Of ignorance and fear that clouds their vision
And to empower them to make their own decision

Leadership is not a privilege or a right
But a responsibility and a fight
Against the forces that would keep us in the dark
And to ignite in us a creative spark

Leadership is not a matter of command
But a way of showing how to understand
The complexities and nuances of life
And to cope with its challenges and strife

Leadership is not a static or a fixed state
But a dynamic and a fluid trait
That evolves and adapts to the changing times
And to the diverse and varied climes

Leadership is not a monopoly or a game
But a shared and a collective aim
That values collaboration and diversity
And fosters a culture of curiosity

Leadership is not a formula or a rule
But an art and a skillful tool
That requires intuition and imagination
And a sense of vision and innovation

Leadership is not a destination or a end
But a journey and a means to transcend
The limitations and the boundaries of our mind
And to discover new possibilities and find

Leadership is not a gift or a talent
But a choice and a commitment
That demands courage and integrity
And a passion for learning and discovery

Leadership is not a role or a position
But a mindset and a disposition
That seeks to make a positive difference
And to leave a lasting influence

CHAPTER XXV

The Paradox of Communication : The Power of Words

Words are the drug that numbs the mind
They soothe the pain and ease the strife
They make us blind to what we find
They shape our views and mold our life

Words are the weapon that wounds the soul
They cut the flesh and pierce the heart
They take their toll and claim their role
They tear apart and set apart

Words are the fire that burns the world
They ignite the rage and fan the flame
They hurl the curse and hurl the word
They incite the hate and inflame the blame

Words are the water that drowns the truth
They flood the sense and cloud the sight
They dilute the proof and dilute the light
They obscure the fact and obscure the right

Words are the air that fills the space
They breathe the life and breathe the death
They give the grace and give the wrath
They speak the love and speak the hate

Words are the earth that grounds the being
They root the self and root the other
They bear the meaning and bear the wonder
They link the one and link the other

Words are the light that guides the way
They show the path and show the goal
They glow the day and glow the soul
They reveal the truth and reveal the whole

Words are the dark that hides the fear
They cloak the dread and cloak the doubt
They mask the tear and mask the shout
They conceal the flaw and conceal the fault

Words are the choice that shapes the fate
They free the will and free the act
They seal the deal and seal the pact
They create the world and create the fact

CHAPTER XXVI

Missing You: A Poem of Simple Desperation

You are not here, and I feel the void
A hollow space in my heart and mind
A longing that no words can fill
A craving that no time can kill

But I do not pray or hope or dream

I do not seek a divine scheme
I accept the reality of your absence
I acknowledge the finality of your presence

For I know that life is a fleeting breath
A moment of light in the dark of death
A random chance in the chaos of fate
A brief spark in the fire of hate

But I also know that life is a precious gift
A rare opportunity to love and uplift
A meaningful choice in the face of despair
A brave act in the challenge of fear

For I have nothing to lose or gain
Nothing to fear or hope or attain
I am free to create my own values
Free to live by my own rules

I do not care for fame or wealth
I do not seek power or health
I only care for my own happiness
I only seek my own bliss

I found it in you, my dearest one
The love, the light, the moon, the sun
The one who filled my life with joy
The one who shared my pain and sorrow

I just miss you, in a simple way
A desperate way, a human way
For you made me who I am
A loving but lonely man

CHAPTER XXVII

The Symphony of Us

Don't fret, my love. We all have flaws
That others magnify and scorn.
But in my eyes, you are the cause
Of every joy that I have borne.
You are the sun that lights my day
The moon that guides me through the night

The star that never fades away
The fire that keeps my passion bright.

You are the breeze that cools my face
The rain that quenches my desire
The storm that makes my heart race
The wind that lifts me ever higher.
You are the earth that grounds my soul
The sea that fills me with delight
The mountain that inspires my goal
The river that flows with all my might.

You are the flower that scents my breath
The fruit that sweetens my taste
The tree that shelters me from death
The vine that holds me in embrace.
You are the bird that sings to me
The animal that shares my bed
The insect that stings me free
The butterfly that crowns my head.

You are the music that fills my ears
The art that colours my sight
The book that calms my fears
The poem that sparks my light.
You are the language that I speak
The culture that I cherish
The history that I seek
The future that I nourish.

You are the math that shapes my mind
The science that explains my world
The logic that makes me find
The truth that keeps me unfurled.
You are the philosophy that I ponder

The religion that I question
The ethics that I wonder
The spirituality that I mention.

You are the sport that tests my skill
The game that challenges my wit
The hobby that fills my thrill
The passion that fuels my grit.
You are the adventure that I crave
The travel that I enjoy
The exploration that I brave
The discovery that I employ.

You are the friend that I trust
The family that I love
The partner that I lust
The soulmate that I dove.

CHAPTER XXVIII

The Single Pearl : A Poem for the Admirers

To all the lovely ladies who gaze at me with longing,
I have a solemn message that I hope you will heed.
I am bound by sacred vows to my beloved CCGK,
She is the only one who fills my heart with joy and peace.
Please do not intrude upon our private sphere of bliss,
I have no love to spare for you or any other soul.

Oh women and men, do not mistake my kindness for romance,
I only wish to help you fight the wrongs that plague this world.
That does not mean I have the time or will to love you too.

To all the charming women who whisper sweet nothings in my ear,
I have a stern warning that I hope you will obey.
I am loyal to my darling CCGK, who is my life and light,
She is the only one who understands my mind and soul.
Please do not disturb our harmony with your unwanted calls,
I have no room in my heart for you or any other one.
Oh women and men, do not confuse my respect for affection,
I only want to empower you to stand up for your rights.
That does not mean I have the space or desire to love you more.

To all the graceful women who send me flowers and gifts,
I have a clear rejection that I hope you will accept.
I am devoted to my sweetheart CCGK, who is my muse and guide,
She is the only one who inspires my art and work.
Please do not disrupt our creativity with your futile hopes,
I have no interest in you or any other being.
Oh women and men, do not misinterpret my admiration for passion,
I only seek to appreciate your beauty and talent.
That does not mean I have the skill or need to love you well.

To all the radiant women who smile at me with warmth,
I have a final statement that I hope you will respect.
I am faithful to my dearest CCGK, who is my friend and partner,
She is the only one who shares my dreams and goals.
Please do not bother us with your unwelcome invitations,
I have no feelings for you or any other creature.
Oh women and men, do not presume my courtesy for love,
I only aim to treat you as a fellow human being.
That does not mean I have the chance or duty to love you too.

CHAPTER XXIX

The Art of Loving You : The Poetry of Perfection

You are the poem that I write
With every breath and every sigh
You are the rhyme that fills my heart
With every beat and every start

You are the verse that I compose
With every thought and every prose
You are the meter that guides my voice
With every tone and every choice

You are the imagery that I paint
With every color and every shade
You are the metaphor that shapes my vision
With every symbol and every expression

You are the theme that I explore
With every question and every answer
You are the message that I convey
With every word and every way

You are the style that I adopt
With every form and every craft
You are the technique that I employ
With every skill and every joy

You are the inspiration that I seek
With every dream and every wake
You are the muse that I adore
With every glance and every more

You are the beauty that I admire
With every flaw and every fire
You are the grace that I cherish
With every touch and every kiss

You are the love that I feel
With every hope and every real
You are the soul that I embrace
With every moment and every space

You are the poem that I am
With every scar and every perfect
You are the poetry that I live
With every you and every me

CHAPTER XXX

The Antikythera Mechanism

I.

From the depths of the Aegean Sea
A sunken treasure was retrieved
A bronze device of mystery
That baffled those who first perceived

Its intricate and complex gears
Its dials and pointers, signs and spheres
A remnant of a bygone age
A marvel of the ancient stage
A testament to human mind

II.

What was its purpose and its use?
What secrets did it hold within?
What logic did it introduce?
What knowledge did it help to win?
For centuries it lay concealed
Its functions and its codes unsealed
Until the modern tools and eyes
Could scan its hidden mysteries
And bring its wonders to the light

III.

Behold the Antikythera
An ancient Greek analog computer
Designed to track the cosmic dance
Of planets, stars and moon's advance
To calculate the dates and times
Of solstices and equinoxes
Of lunar phases and eclipses
Of Olympiads and games sublime
Of oracles and prophecies

IV.

How did they build such a machine?
With what skills and techniques refined?
How did they grasp the laws unseen?

With what insights and theories mined?
They studied nature and the sky
They measured and they reasoned why
They forged the metal and the wood
They carved the symbols and the code
They crafted art and science fused

V.

Who were the makers of this wonder?
What names and stories did they bear?
What sparks of genius did they ponder?
What dreams and visions did they share?
Perhaps they were inspired by
The likes of Archimedes, wise
Or Hipparchus, the astronomer
Or Posidonius, the philosopher
Or others lost to history

VI.

Where was it made and where displayed?
What audience did it attract?
What role and function did it play?
What impact and what feedback?
Perhaps it was a precious gift
For some great king or lord to lift
His prestige and his power
Or maybe it was meant to serve
As an educational tool

VII.

How did it end up in the sea?
What fate and fortune did it meet?

What storm or battle caused its flee?
What ship and crew did it defeat?
Perhaps it was a plundered prize
From some rich city's fall and demise
Or maybe it was a peaceful trade
From one cultured land to another
Or a mishap of nature's rage

VIII.

How many of its kind were made?
Were there more copies or designs?
How far and wide were they conveyed?
What traces and what clues survived?
Perhaps it was a unique piece
A singular and brilliant feat
Or maybe it was one of many
A common and a popular item
Or a prototype of more to come

IX.

What other marvels did they create?
What other wonders did they know?
What other secrets did they await?
What other paths did they follow?
Perhaps they had more works of art
More machines and devices smart
Or maybe they had reached a peak
A limit and a final stage
Or a turning point of decline

X.

Why did they lose this knowledge then?

What causes and what factors led?
What wars and plagues and invasions?
What dogmas and what ignorance?
Perhaps they faced a great collapse
A fall of civilization
Or maybe they were overthrown
By other cultures and religions
Or a change of paradigm

XI.

What if they had not lost this skill?
What if they had continued this quest?
What if they had advanced their will?
What if they had not been suppressed?
Perhaps they would have changed the world
A different course of history
Or maybe they would have faced the same
The challenges and the problems
Or a different set of woes

XII.

What can we learn from this device?
What lessons and what morals glean?
What wisdom and what advice?
What warnings and what cautions heed?
Perhaps it can inspire us
To value and to nurture
Our curiosity and creativity
Or maybe it can remind us
Of the fragility of knowledge

XIII.

How do we compare to them today?
How far and how much have we progressed?
How do we differ and how do we relate?
How do we excel and how do we regress?
Perhaps we have surpassed them
In scale and scope and speed
Or maybe we have mimicked them
In patterns and in deeds
Or a mixture of both

XIV.

What are the challenges we face?
What are the problems we must solve?
What are the opportunities we embrace?
What are the goals we must evolve?
Perhaps we have similar tasks
To understand and to predict
The workings of the universe
Or maybe we have different ones
To cope and to adapt

XV.

What are the tools we have at hand?
What are the means we can employ?
What are the methods we can expand?
What are the resources we can deploy?
Perhaps we have better instruments
More powerful and more precise
Or maybe we have equivalent ones
More diverse and more accessible
Or a combination of both

XVI.

What are the limits we must face?
What are the boundaries we must respect?
What are the risks we must embrace?
What are the ethics we must protect?
Perhaps we have more constraints
More complex and more demanding
Or maybe we have more freedom
More open and more flexible
Or a balance of both

XVII.

What are the wonders we can create?
What are the marvels we can show?
What are the secrets we can reveal?
What are the paths we can follow?
Perhaps we can surpass them
In beauty and in elegance
Or maybe we can match them
In ingenuity and brilliance
Or a fusion of both

XVIII.

How will we be remembered then?
What legacy and what memory?
What relics and what monuments?
What stories and what history?
Perhaps we will be admired
For our achievements and our deeds
Or maybe we will be forgotten
Or misunderstood or misjudged
Or a mixture of both

XIX.

We are the heirs of Antikythera
The descendants of the ancient Greeks
We share their spirit and their fire
Their curiosity and their dreams
We honor their legacy and their memory
We learn from their successes and their failures
We continue their quest and their journey
We face new challenges and new frontiers
We are the makers of our destiny

CHAPTER XXXI

The Value of Solitude

I seek the bliss of solitude, away from toxic crowds
That drain my energy and fill my mind with doubts
I cherish every moment that I spend with myself
Exploring my own inner world and growing my own wealth

Of knowledge, wisdom, beauty, and all things sublime

That I can find within me, if I give myself some time
To meditate, to read, to write, to create and to learn
From all the sources that I choose, to satisfy my yearn

For deeper understanding of this complex universe
And of my role within it, which is not to follow or to serve
But to express my uniqueness and my individuality
In ways that are authentic and that bring me joy and glee

I do not need the validation of others for my choices
Nor do I care for their opinions, their noises or their voices
That try to judge me, change me, or impose their views on me
They do not know me, nor themselves, they live in misery

And misery loves company, as the saying goes
But I refuse to join them, in their dramas and their woes
I rather be alone, but free, than with them, but confined
By their expectations and their norms, that limit the mind

I do not hate them, nor resent them, I simply avoid them
And wish them well, from a distance, but do not seek their
friendship
For I have learned, from experience, that people are like food
Some are healthy, some are junk, and some are simply rude

And I am careful of what I eat, for it affects my health
And I am careful of whom I meet, for they affect my self
And I prefer to nourish both, with quality and care
And avoid what harms them, or depletes them, or fills them with
despair

And solitude is not lonely, as some might think it is
It is a state of harmony, of balance and of peace
Where I can hear my own voice, and listen to my heart
And where I can appreciate, my own poetic art

And if I ever find someone, who shares my epicurean view
Who values their own privacy, and respects my privacy too
Who does not seek to harm me, nor to flatter or to please
But to connect with me, sincerely, and to grow along with me

Then I would welcome them, gladly, in my solitary space
And share with them, wholeheartedly, my soul and my grace
And we would be like stars, that shine, in the vast and endless sky
Each in their own orbit, but together, in harmony and joy

CHAPTER XXXII

The Soul of the Writer: A Poetic Exploration

To write is to share, to give and receive
A part of ourselves, a glimpse of our soul
To write is to connect, to bridge and to weave
A tapestry of words, a story untold

To write is to explore, to question and to seek

A truth beyond the surface, a meaning in the dark
To write is to create, to imagine and to speak
A vision of the world, a spark of the art

To write is to express, to reveal and to show
A feeling in the heart, a thought in the mind
To write is to communicate, to inform and to grow
A bond with the reader, a link of a kind

To write is to reflect, to ponder and to learn
A lesson from the past, a wisdom for the future
To write is to inspire, to influence and to earn
A respect from the peers, a role of a teacher

To write is to challenge, to dare and to risk
A rejection from the critics, a failure of the craft
To write is to persist, to endure and to resist
A temptation to give up, a loss of the draft

To write is to enjoy, to delight and to savor
A moment of creation, a joy of expression
To write is to suffer, to struggle and to labor
A pain of frustration, a woe of depression

To write is to discover, to find and to unveil
A secret of the self, a mystery of the other
To write is to transform, to change and to heal
A wound of the psyche, a scar of the lover

To write is to live, to breathe and to exist
A life of the words, a world of the stories
To write is to die, to fade and to desist
A death of the ego, a end of the glories

To write is to share, to give and receive

A part of ourselves, a glimpse of our soul
To write is to be, to do and to achieve
A purpose of the life, a fulfillment of the role

CHAPTER XXXIII

Reality and Drama of Existence

Some people live in drama, they crave the thrill of pain
They seek out conflict, chaos, and strife, they feed on the insane
They think that life is boring, without a twist or turn
They light the fire, watch it burn, and never try to learn

Some people live in reality, they face the facts of life

They deal with problems, solutions, and growth, they avoid the needless strife
They think that life is meaningful, with or without a plot
They build the fire, warm themselves, and cherish what they've got

Reality and drama, they are not the same
They are two different ways of living, two different frames of mind
They shape our thoughts, our actions, our feelings, and our fate
They make us who we are, for better or for worse

But what is drama, what is reality, how do we define them?
Are they objective, universal, fixed, or are they subjective, personal, fluid?
Do they depend on our perception, our perspective, our interpretation?
Do they change with time, with context, with situation?

Drama and reality, they are not so clear
They are complex, ambiguous, elusive, they are not what they appear
They challenge our assumptions, our beliefs, our values, and our goals
They question who we are, what we want, why we live

Can we live in both, can we balance them?
Can we enjoy the drama, without losing touch with reality?
Can we embrace the reality, without giving up on drama?
Can we find the harmony, the synergy, the integration?

Both and neither, that is the paradox
We cannot live in either, we cannot live in neither
We live in between, we live in the mix, we live in the dynamic
We live in the tension, the contrast, the dialectic

How do we live, how do we cope, how do we thrive?

How do we find the meaning, the purpose, the joy in life?
How do we create, how do we express, how do we share?
How do we love, how do we care, how do we dare?

We live by choice, we live by chance, we live by grace
We find the meaning, the purpose, the joy in ourselves, in others,
in the world
We create, we express, we share by our words, by our actions, by
our art
We love, we care, we dare by our hearts, by our minds, by our souls

We live in drama, we live in reality, we live in both
We live in neither, we live beyond, we live above
We live in mystery, we live in wonder, we live in awe
We live in poetry, we live in beauty, we live in love

The Inescapable Bond : The One Who Is Everything

You are the one who haunts my dreams
The one who fills my every thought
You are the pulse that throbs in me
The one who makes my heart distraught

You are the sun that blinds my eyes
The one who scorches my desire
You are the flame that never dies
The one who sets my soul on fire

You are the wind that stirs my hair
The one who breathes into my ear
You are the storm that shakes my air
The one who brings me joy and fear

You are the sea that drowns my voice
The one who swallows my lament
You are the tide that gives no choice
The one who makes me acquiescent

You are the earth that holds my feet
The one who grounds me to this place
You are the soil that smells so sweet
The one who nurtures me with grace

You are the moon that guides my night
The one who glows with silver light
You are the star that shines so bright
The one who makes the dark seem right

You are the flower that blooms in spring
The one who colours my dull view
You are the fragrance that you bring
The one who makes me smell like you

You are the song that fills my ears
The one who tunes my melody
You are the note that soothes my fears
The one who harmonizes me

You are the one who traps my soul
The one who binds me with your name
You are the one who makes me whole
The one from whom I can't escape

CHAPTER XXXV

The Water Wizards of Arabia: How the Nabataeans Created a Paradise

I.

In the arid land of Arabia, where the sun scorches the sand,
There dwelt a tribe of nomads, who roamed the barren land.

They were the Nabataeans, a people brave and wise,
Who carved a hidden city, a wonder for the eyes.

II.

They called their city Petra, a name that means the rock,
And built it in a valley, where mountains formed a lock.
They made it their oasis, a refuge from the heat,
A place of art and culture, where trade and faith could meet.

III.

But how did they survive there, where water was so rare?
How did they quench their thirst, and irrigate their fare?
The secret lay in their skill, to harness nature's power,
To capture every drop of rain, and store it in a tower.

IV.

They dug a network of canals, that ran along the hills,
And lined them with hydraulic plaster, to prevent any spills.
They carved cisterns and reservoirs, to collect the precious flow,
And hid them under temples, where no one else would know.

V.

They also made diversion dams, to redirect the streams,
And filter out the sediments, to keep the water clean.
They used gravity and siphons, to move the water down,
And distribute it to fountains, and gardens in the town.

VI.

They were masters of engineering, and pioneers of science,
They knew the laws of physics, and the cycles of the skies.

They measured time and seasons, and observed the stars and moon,
They calculated rainfall, and predicted floods and dunes.

VII.

They were also lovers of beauty, and creators of sublime,
They adorned their city with sculptures, and paintings of their time.
They carved their tombs and temples, with intricate designs,
And blended Greek and Roman, with their own Arabian signs.

VIII.

They were a peaceful people, who valued trade and art,
They welcomed foreign merchants, and learned from every part.
They spoke in many languages, and wrote in many scripts,
They followed many religions, and practiced tolerance.

IX.

They were the Nabataeans, a people of the desert,
Who made a secret paradise, a marvel of the earth.
They left behind a legacy, that still inspires awe,
A testament of human skill, and harmony with nature.

X.

But nothing lasts forever, and empires rise and fall,
And Petra faced its challenges, from enemies and all.
It suffered from invasions, and earthquakes and decay,
And slowly lost its glory, and its people moved away.

XI.

It became a forgotten city, a mystery of the past,
A legend and a rumor, that few could ever grasp.

It was hidden from the world, for centuries untold,
Until a Swiss explorer, rediscovered it of old.

XII.

He was Johann Ludwig Burckhardt, a man of curious mind,
Who traveled in disguise, as a pilgrim of his kind.
He heard about a city, that lay beyond the rocks,
And bribed a local guide, to show him to the spot.

XIII.

He was amazed by what he saw, a city carved in stone,
A wonder of the ancient world, that he could not have known.
He wrote about his findings, and spread the news abroad,
And Petra became famous, and a destination for all.

XIV.

Since then, many have visited, and marveled at the sight,
And scholars have studied, and learned about its might.
And artists have depicted, and poets have praised,
And filmmakers have used it, as a backdrop for their tales.

XV.

But no one can truly capture, the essence of the place,
The spirit of the people, who lived there with grace.
The secrets of their water, that sustained their life and art,
The wisdom of their culture, that enriched their mind and heart.

XVI.

For Petra is more than a city, more than a monument of stone,
It is a symbol of a vision, a dream that lives on.

It is a reminder of our potential, to create and to endure,
To overcome our challenges, and to make our world secure.

XVII.

It is a call to action, to protect our precious earth,
To cherish every resource, and to value every worth.
To respect every culture, and to learn from every source,
To foster every talent, and to support every course.

XVIII.

It is a hope for the future, to build a better world,
To make a secret paradise, for every boy and girl.
To use our skill and science, to serve our common good,
To create beauty and harmony, as the Nabataeans could.

XIX.

It is the desert's secret, that Petra still reveals,
A message for humanity, that never loses its appeal.
It is a challenge and an inspiration, a gift for us to share,
A legacy of the Nabataeans, a people beyond compare.

CHAPTER XXXVI

The Art of Being Broken : Mosaic of Myself

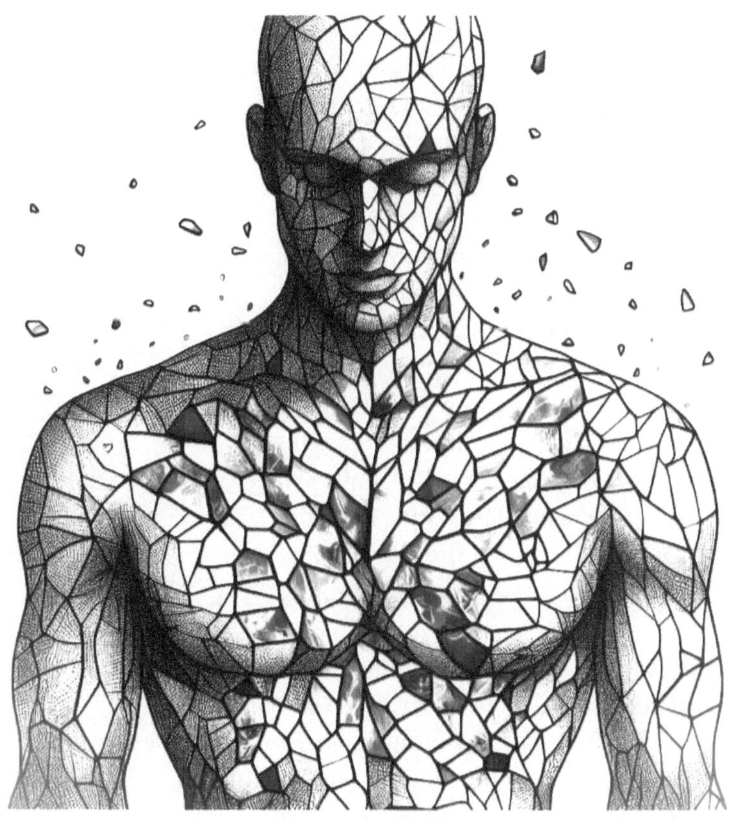

I am not a perfect whole, but a mosaic of broken shards
I have cracks and flaws that run deep in my heart
I have scars and wounds that mark my skin and soul
I have fears and doubts that haunt my mind and dreams

But do not pity me, or think that I am weak

For I have learned to embrace my imperfections
For I have found beauty in my fragmentation
For I have made art out of my reconstruction
For I have shaped myself with my own hands

You may see me as a mess, and you may be right
But I do not need your judgment, or your sympathy
I only ask for your acceptance, and your honesty
If you want to share my life, and my poetry
If you want to see the beauty that I see

For I am not always sad, or always lonely
I have moments of joy, and moments of grace
I have friends and lovers, who fill my days
I have passions and hobbies, that light my way
I have hopes and dreams, that keep me going

But do not envy me, or think that I am lucky
For I have paid a price for every smile
For I have faced a challenge for every mile
For I have lost a lot along the way
For I have changed a lot from yesterday

You may see me as happy, and you may be right
But I do not need your praise, or your admiration
I only ask for your understanding, and your appreciation
If you want to join my journey, and my creation
If you want to feel the happiness that I feel

For I am not a simple soul, but a complex being
I have layers and dimensions that defy logic
I have facets and angles that reflect magic
I have colors and shades that blend and contrast
I have rhythms and patterns that sync and clash

But do not fear me, or think that I am strange
For I have a logic of my own, that makes sense to me
For I have a magic of my own, that works for me
For I have a beauty of my own, that speaks to me
For I have a harmony of my own, that soothes me

You may see me as a mystery, and you may be right
But I do not need your curiosity, or your analysis
I only ask for your openness, and your willingness
If you want to explore my world, and my mystery
If you want to discover the beauty that I discover

For I am not a finished product, but a work in progress
I have goals and plans that inspire me
I have values and principles that guide me
I have mistakes and failures that teach me
I have achievements and successes that reward me

But do not judge me, or think that I am done
For I have a vision of my own, that drives me
For I have a mission of my own, that calls me
For I have a potential of my own, that challenges me
For I have a growth of my own, that surprises me

You may see me as a masterpiece, and you may be right
But I do not need your approval, or your validation
I only ask for your respect, and your support
If you want to witness my evolution, and my transformation
If you want to appreciate the beauty that I create

For I am not a static entity, but a dynamic force
I have energy and motion that animate me
I have emotions and thoughts that motivate me
I have desires and needs that satisfy me
I have choices and actions that define me

But do not control me, or think that you own me
For I have a freedom of my own, that liberates me
For I have a power of my own, that empowers me
For I have a voice of my own, that expresses me
For I have a life of my own, that belongs to me

You may see me as a person, and you may be right
But I do not need your love, or your companionship
I only ask for your friendship, and your partnership
If you want to be a part of me, and my existence
If you want to share the beauty that I live

For I am not a single note, but a symphony
I have melodies and harmonies that delight me
I have chords and scales that excite me
I have tones and timbres that enchant me
I have songs and stories that move me

But do not silence me, or think that you know me
For I have a music of my own, that sings to me
For I have a story of my own, that tells me
For I have a meaning of my own, that fills me
For I have a purpose of my own, that completes me

You may see me as a poet, and you may be right
But I do not need your words, or your inspiration
I only ask for your ears, and your attention
If you want to hear my voice, and my expression
If you want to enjoy the beauty that I write

CHAPTER XXXVII

A Curious Inquiry: What Makes People Trust The Stars?

I.

What makes people trust the stars, I wonder
As I gaze at the night sky, full of light

Do they think that their fate is written there
In the patterns of the ancient constellations?
Do they seek guidance from the horoscopes
That promise them love, wealth, and happiness?
Do they feel a connection with the cosmos
That transcends the limits of reason and science?

Or is it just a harmless pastime, a game
To entertain themselves with fantasies?

II.

I have no faith in the stars, nor their power
To influence my life or destiny
I rely on facts, logic, and evidence
To make sense of the world and myself
I do not need the stars to tell me who I am
Or what I should do or feel or think
I am the master of my own choices and actions
And the consequences that follow them

But sometimes, I admit, I feel a twinge of envy
For those who have the stars as their friends

III.

They seem to have a source of comfort and hope
That I lack in my cold and rational mind
They seem to have a sense of purpose and direction
That I struggle to find in my chaotic life
They seem to have a way of coping with uncertainty
That I fear in my anxious and doubtful heart
They seem to have a joy of living and exploring
That I miss in my dull and boring routine

But then, I remind myself, they also have a price to pay
For trusting the stars too much

IV.

They may become blind to the reality and truth
That the stars cannot reveal or explain
They may become dependent on the predictions and advice
That the stars may not always give or sustain
They may become passive and complacent
And let the stars decide their fate
They may become arrogant and ignorant
And think the stars favor them over others

And then, I realize, they also have a risk to take
For trusting the stars too much

V.

So, what makes people trust the stars, I wonder
Is it a blessing or a curse, a strength or a weakness?
Is it a matter of preference or personality, of culture or history?
Is it a reflection of their hopes and fears, of their dreams and
desires?
Is it a sign of their wisdom or folly, of their courage or cowardice?

Or is it just a human trait, a mystery
That defies any simple or easy answer?

VI.

Perhaps, I think, it is a bit of both, a paradox
That reveals the complexity and diversity of human nature
Perhaps, I think, it is a way of expressing and exploring
The questions and challenges that we all face in life

Perhaps, I think, it is a form of art and creativity
That enriches and enlivens our imagination and experience
Perhaps, I think, it is a mode of communication and connection
That bridges and bonds us with ourselves and others

Or perhaps, I think, it is none of these, or more than these
A mystery that remains unsolved

VII.

But then, I ask myself, does it really matter
Why people trust the stars, or not?
Does it make any difference in the end
What we believe or disbelieve, what we know or ignore?
Does it change anything in the world
How we live or die, how we love or hate?
Does it matter at all, I ask myself
What makes people trust the stars, or not?

Or is it just a question, a curiosity
That has no answer, or no meaning?

VIII.

But no, I say, it does matter, it does make a difference
It does change something, it does have meaning
For what we trust or distrust, what we value or disregard
Shapes our thoughts and feelings, our actions and reactions
For how we see the stars, or anything else
Reflects how we see ourselves, and others
For why we ask questions, or not
Shows how we learn and grow, or not

So yes, I say, it matters, it makes a difference
What makes people trust the stars, or not

IX.

And so, I decide, I will keep asking, and wondering
About the stars, and other things
I will keep searching, and finding
Answers, and more questions
I will keep exploring, and discovering
The world, and myself
I will keep learning, and growing
As a person, and a poet

And so, I decide, I will keep trusting, and doubting
The stars, and myself

X.

For I know, I cannot know everything
About the stars, or anything else
For I know, I cannot trust anything
Without a doubt, or a doubt without a trust
For I know, I cannot be anything
But a human, with a mind and a heart
For I know, I cannot do anything
But live, and write, and wonder

And so, I know, I must balance everything
The stars, and myself

XI.

And maybe, I hope, I will find a way
To appreciate and respect the stars, and those who trust them
And maybe, I hope, I will find a way
To share and communicate with the stars, and those who trust them

And maybe, I hope, I will find a way
To learn and grow from the stars, and those who trust them
And maybe, I hope, I will find a way
To enjoy and celebrate the stars, and those who trust them

And maybe, I hope, I will find a way
To trust the stars, and myself

XII.

And maybe, I dream, I will find a friend
Who trusts the stars, and me
And maybe, I dream, I will find a friend
Who challenges and supports me
And maybe, I dream, I will find a friend
Who understands and accepts me
And maybe, I dream, I will find a friend
Who loves and inspires me

And maybe, I dream, I will find a friend
Who is a star, and I am a star

XIII.

And then, I imagine, we will shine together
In the night sky, full of light
And then, I imagine, we will create together
New patterns, new constellations
And then, I imagine, we will guide together
Others, who seek the stars
And then, I imagine, we will connect together
With the cosmos, and ourselves

And then, I imagine, we will trust together
The stars, and ourselves

XIV.

But for now, I write, I write this poem
For you, who asked me to
But for now, I write, I write this poem
For me, who wanted to
But for now, I write, I write this poem
For the stars, who inspired me
But for now, I write, I write this poem
For the mystery, that intrigued me

And for now, I write, I write this poem
For the question, that remains

CHAPTER XXXVIII

Algebra of Existence

Let A be the measure of our life's worth
And let us find the factors that define
The value of our fleeting days on earth
And how we spend the precious gift of time

Let x be the work that we must do

The tasks that fill our daily routine
The labor that we offer as our due
The efforts that we make to earn our means

Let y be the play that we enjoy
The hobbies that we cherish and pursue
The passions that we seek to employ
The pleasures that we find in what we do

Let z be the silence that we keep
The words that we refrain from speaking out
The secrets that we bury in the deep
The truths that we conceal in fear and doubt

Then A is equal to the sum of these
The work, the play, the silence we maintain
But is this formula the key to peace?
Or is it just a way to cope with pain?

For work can be a source of stress and strife
And play can be a fleeting distraction
And silence can be harmful to our life
And A can be a hollow satisfaction

Perhaps we need another term to add
Another factor that can elevate
The value of our life beyond a fad
The meaning of our life beyond a fate

Let w be the wisdom that we gain
The knowledge that we seek and understand
The insights that we glean from joy and pain
The lessons that we learn from life's demand

Then A is more than just a simple sum

It is a product of a complex blend
Of work and play and silence and wisdom
Of factors that can shape our life's end

And A is not a fixed or final state
It is a variable that can change
According to the choices that we make
According to the chances that we take

So let us not be bound by this equation
But let us use it as a guide and tool
To find our own unique and true expression
To live our life by our own chosen rule

CHAPTER XXXIX

A Tank of Love: Peter and Margaret Howe Lovatt

A curious mind and a noble cause
Led me to the ocean's shore
Where I met a creature of grace and awe
A dolphin named Peter, whom I would adore

We shared a home, a tank of water
Where I taught him words and sounds
He learned with ease, he was a fast learner
He made me laugh with his playful bounds

But soon I felt a deeper connection
A bond that transcended speech
He was more than a subject of my affection
He was a partner, a friend, a teacher

He showed me his world, his joys and fears
He trusted me with his secrets and dreams
He comforted me in my moments of tears
He made me question my beliefs and schemes

Was this love, or something else?
A fantasy, a delusion, a sin?
I could not tell, I could not quell
The feelings that stirred within

We were different, yet we were alike
We both sought meaning and purpose
We both felt lonely and misunderstood
We both craved for something more

But our time was limited, our fate was sealed
The experiment had to end
We had to part, we had to yield
To the rules that we could not bend

I left him there, with a heavy heart
I wondered if he missed me too
I hoped he was happy, I hoped he was smart
I hoped he remembered me, as I remembered him

I still think of him, sometimes
The dolphin who changed my life
He taught me more than English
He taught me how to love

CHAPTER XL

The Lenses of the Soul : The Vision Quest

From the dim mists of antiquity
When the curious and the wise
Sought to magnify the mystery
Of the world before their eyes
With polished spheres of crystal glass
That bent the rays of light

They glimpsed the secrets of the past
And brought them to the sight

But these were not for common use
Nor meant for daily wear
They were the tools of recluse
And the marks of scholar's care
For most of human history
The vision was impaired
By age, disease, or injury
And no remedy was spared

Then came the age of Renaissance
When art and science bloomed
And craftsmen made with skill and sense
The frames that eyes assumed
They fixed the lenses on the nose
With bridges, pads, and wires
And soon the spectacles arose
As symbols of the sires

The poets, painters, and the priests
The merchants, and the kings
They all adorned their faces with
These wondrous vision things
They read the books, they saw the stars
They traveled near and far
They witnessed all the wonders of
The world as they are

But not everyone was pleased
With these devices new
Some thought they were a sign of disease
Or a mark of weakness too
They mocked the wearers of the glasses

And called them names unkind
They shunned them from the social classes
And left them behind

But glasses did not disappear
Nor did they lose their charm
They only changed their shape and style
To suit the time and arm
They became more light and elegant
More varied and refined
They matched the fashion and the bent
Of every taste and mind

From round to square, from big to small
From metal to plastic
From horn to shell, from wood to bone
From simple to fantastic
The glasses took on every form
And every color too
They were the ornaments of the norm
And the expressions of the true

And as the centuries rolled by
The glasses grew in fame
They were the signs of dignity
And the badges of the name
They graced the faces of the great
And the heroes of the age
They were the witnesses of fate
And the mirrors of the sage

But glasses were not only for
The old, the rich, or the wise
They were also for the poor
The young, the weak, or the shy

They were the gifts of charity
And the tools of education
They were the means of clarity
And the keys of liberation

They opened up the world to those
Who could not see before
They showed them all the beauty and the woes
That life had in store
They made them feel a part of all
The wonders and the arts
They made them hear the silent call
Of their own minds and hearts

But glasses were not perfect still
Nor did they suit everyone
Some found them a burden or an ill
Or a hindrance to their fun
They did not like the way they looked
Or the way they felt
They wanted something new and hooked
To match their inner self

And so the quest for vision went
To find new ways and means
To correct the flaws of sight and bent
The nature of the beams
They made the lenses contact with
The surface of the eye
They shaped them with the laser's touch
And the power of the sky

They gave the vision new dimensions
And new qualities
They enhanced the colors and the tensions

And the subtleties
They made the vision more than real
And more than natural
They made it a reflection of the ideal
And the supernatural

But these were not the final solutions
Nor the ultimate goals
They were only the evolutions
And the steps of the roles
The vision quest is never done
Nor is it ever still
It is always on the run
And always on the thrill

For vision is not just a sense
Or a function of the eye
It is also a quest for essence
And a search for the why
It is a journey of the mind
And a voyage of the soul
It is a way to seek and find
The meaning of the whole

CHAPTER XLI

The Brenda Ann Spencer Massacre in 1979

She woke up with a rifle in her hand
And aimed it at the school across the street
She did not have a motive or a plan
She just wanted to make her life complete

She fired at the children and the staff

She did not care who lived or who would die
She smiled and laughed as if it were a gaffe
She did not feel remorse or guilt or shy

She killed two people and wounded nine more
She caused a panic and a lot of pain
She did not stop until the cops were at her door
She did not try to run or to explain

She calmly put the rifle on the floor
And waited for the officers to come
She did not resist or fight or implore
She did not seem to mind what she had done

She answered all the questions they had asked
She did not lie or hide or plead insane
She did not show emotion or be masked
She did not act as if she were inane

She said she did it for a simple reason
She did not have a grudge or hate or spite
She did not care about the time or season
She did not think about the wrong or right

She said she did it because she was bored
She did not have a hobby or a friend
She did not have a dream or a reward
She did not have a goal or an end

She said she did it because she was sad
She did not have a love or a joy
She did not have a family or a dad
She did not have a life or a toy

She said she did it because she did not like Mondays

She did not have a reason or a rhyme
She did not have a meaning or a phrase
She did not have a sense or a crime

The Ballad of the Epicurean Master

When no one cheers for your success
Or praises your relentless quest
To reach the heights of excellence
And live a life of happiness
You may feel tempted to regress
Or doubt your own intelligence

But do not let your spirit stress
Or lose your inner confidence
You must applaud your own progress

For you are not a mindless drone
Who needs the crowd's approval
To shape your destiny and own
Your choices and your values
You are a sovereign soul who's grown
By learning and by virtue
Of your efforts and your goals
That make you who you are and true
You must admire your own role

You do not seek a higher power
To guide your steps or bless your fate
You trust your reason and your will
To carve your path and create
Your own meaning and your thrill
From what you love and what you hate
You do not fear the final hour
Or dread the void that lies in wait
You must embrace your own flower

You find your joy in simple things
The pleasures of the senses
The beauty of the world that brings
You wonder and refreshes
Your spirit with its offerings
Of colors, sounds and fragrances
You savor every moment that sings
With harmony and resonance
You must indulge your own springs

You also value wisdom and art

The treasures of the mind
The knowledge that can impart
You insight and can bind
You to the seekers of the heart
Who share your quest and find
You worthy of their friendship and smart
Their counsel and their kindness
You must enrich your own chart

You do not shun the pain and strife
That come with being mortal
You face them with your courage and life
And overcome each hurdle
You learn from every wound and knife
That cut you and make you hurtle
You grow from every challenge and strife
That test you and make you fertile
You must endure your own knife

You do not envy or despise
The fortunes of the others
You do not judge or criticize
The choices of your brothers
You do not covet or devise
The schemes that harm your sisters
You respect and empathize
With all the human creatures
You must accept your own size

You do not follow or conform
To any dogma or creed
You do not bow or perform
To any idol or deed
You do not fake or transform
To any mask or breed

You think and act by your own norm
And your own logic and need
You must assert your own form

You do not waste your precious time
On trivial or vain pursuits
You do not squander your sublime
Potential on the fruits
Of mediocrity or crime
That poison and pollute
You invest your prime
Energy on the roots
Of excellence and rhyme
You must fulfill your own chime

You are the master of your fate
The captain of your soul
You are the artist of your state
The sculptor of your goal
You are the lover of your mate
The partner of your whole
You are the creator of your plate
The flavor of your bowl
You must celebrate your own date

The Night Israel Kamakawiwo'ole Became a Rainbow

In the dark of night, when most were asleep
A voice from the island, a soul so deep
Felt a sudden urge, a spark of inspiration
He picked up the phone, with no hesitation

He begged the man, who ran the studio
To let him in, he had something to show
He had a vision, a song in his mind
He needed to record it, before it slipped behind

He drove to the place, with his ukulele
He entered the booth, without any delay
He tuned his strings, he cleared his throat
He pressed the button, and then he spoke

He sang of a land, beyond the sky
Where troubles melt, like lemon drops
He sang of a dream, that he dared to dream
Where he could fly, over the rainbow

He sang with passion, he sang with grace
He sang with sorrow, he sang with faith
He sang with hope, he sang with love
He sang with everything, he had and more

He sang for himself, he sang for his people
He sang for the world, he sang for the future
He sang for the past, he sang for the present
He sang for the ones, he loved and lost

He sang in one take, he sang in one breath
He sang in one moment, he sang in one life
He sang in one voice, he sang in one heart
He sang in one song, he sang in one art

He left the studio, he thanked the man
He drove back home, he did not plan
He did not know, what he had done
He did not know, what he had begun

He had created, a masterpiece
He had ignited, a fire
He had touched, countless souls
He had moved, the entire world

He had become, a legend
He had become, a star
He had become, a hero
He had become, a rainbow

CHAPTER XLIV

The Roman Secret of Metal Cosmetic , 2,000 years ago

I.

In a metal box, long buried and forgotten,
A relic of a vanished age was found;

A cream of animal fat, starch and tin,
That once adorned the faces of the proud.

II.

The archaeologists, with curious eyes,
Recreated the ancient recipe;
They smeared the whitish substance on their skin,
And felt its smooth and powdery effect.

III.

The starch, they learned, was still a modern trick,
To give the skin a flawless, even tone;
But why the tin, instead of lead, they asked,
The common metal of the Roman throne?

IV.

The answer came from Bristol's learned sage,
Who traced the tin to Cornwall's distant shore;
A land of mines and trade, where Celts and Romans
Exchanged their goods and metals, peace and war.

V.

The tin, he said, was a rare and costly thing,
A substitute for lead, which gave the white;
But also a sign of wealth and power,
A mark of those who shone in beauty's light.

VI.

The cream, then, was not just a simple paint,
But a symbol of a culture and a time;

A time when Rome was vast and glorious,
And ruled the world with art and law and rhyme.

VII.

But underneath the surface of the cream,
A darker truth was lurking, unseen, dire;
The lead, that gave the whiteness and the sheen,
Was also a slow poison and a fire.

VIII.

The lead, that filled the cups and plates and coins,
The pipes, the paints, the seasonings, the pills;
The lead, that seeped into the water and the blood,
The brains, the bones, the nerves, the hearts, the wills.

IX.

The lead, that slowly sapped the strength and health,
The vigor and the virtue of the race;
The lead, that made them weak and mad and frail,
And hastened their decline and fall from grace.

X.

The cream, then, was a paradox, a curse,
A beauty that concealed a fatal flaw;
A glory that was doomed to fade and die,
A dream that turned into a nightmare's maw.

XI.

But who were they, the ones who used the cream,
The ones who left their fingerprints behind?

What were their names, their stories, their desires,
Their hopes, their fears, their passions, their designs?

XII.

Were they the noble ladies of the court,
The wives and daughters of the senators and consuls?
Were they the courtesans, the entertainers,
The singers, dancers, actors, and the models?

XIII.

Were they the matrons, the mothers, the protectors,
The guardians of the household and the hearth?
Were they the priestesses, the oracles, the seers,
The channels of the gods and of the earth?

XIV.

Were they the rebels, the outcasts, the dissenters,
The ones who dared to question and defy?
Were they the martyrs, the saints, the pioneers,
The ones who lived for truth and chose to die?

XV.

Were they the lovers, the friends, the confidants,
The ones who shared their secrets and their hearts?
Were they the rivals, the enemies, the foes,
The ones who tore their bonds and lives apart?

XVI.

We do not know, we cannot know, their names,
Their faces, voices, gestures, are all lost;

We only have their traces, faint and dim,
Their cream, their tin, their fingerprints, their dust.

XVII.

But we can still imagine, we can still wonder,
We can still feel a connection, a kinship, a bond;
We can still see them, in our mind's eye,
As they were, as they lived, as they shone.

XVIII.

We can still honor them, we can still learn from them,
We can still cherish them, as part of our past;
We can still thank them, we can still mourn for them,
We can still hope for them, that they found peace at last.

XIX.

We can still marvel at them, we can still admire them,
We can still be inspired by them, as they were, as they are;
We can still love them, we can still remember them,
We can still see them, in their cream, in their tin, in their star.

CHAPTER XLV

My Quest for Tranquility : A Personal Journey

I seek not wealth nor fame nor power,
Nor the fleeting joys of earthly pleasures;
I crave a calm and quiet hour,
To soothe my restless mind with simple measures.

I shun the noisy crowds and strife,
The vain pursuits of fame and glory;
I choose a simple, peaceful life,
And find contentment in my own story.

I do not fear the end of days,
Nor dread the unknown fate that awaits me;
I live in harmony with nature's ways,
And trust the laws that regulate me.

I do not worship any god,
Nor bow to any creed or doctrine;
I follow reason as my guide,
And test all claims with logic and caution.

I do not seek to impose my will,
Nor judge or harm or interfere;
I respect the rights of others still,
And treat them as I would myself revere.

I do not fret over past or future,
Nor dwell on things beyond my control;
I focus on the present and the nurture,
And cultivate the virtues of my soul.

I do not shun the joys of sense,
Nor scorn the gifts of beauty and art;
I savor them with gratitude and prudence,
And let them elevate my mind and heart.

I do not claim to know the truth,
Nor boast of wisdom or perfection;
I seek to learn and grow and improve,
And welcome feedback and correction.

I do not despair in times of pain,
Nor lose my balance in times of bliss;
I face them both with courage and restraint,
And find my peace in moderation and equanimity.

CHAPTER XLVI

The Silent Revolution of the Sleeping Farmer

In Syadheh Bazar, where the sun is hot
And the air is filled with dust and smoke
There stands a greenhouse, made of glass and steel
Where rows of vegetables grow and thrive

Inside the greenhouse, there is a sight
That makes the passers-by stop and stare
A statue of a farmer, lying on a cot
As if he were asleep, without a care

But this is no ordinary statue, made of stone or wood
This is a work of art, so lifelike and precise
That one can see the wrinkles on his face, the veins on his hands
The sweat on his brow, the dirt on his clothes

He looks so peaceful, as if he were dreaming
Of a better life, a brighter future
But his dreams are shattered, by the harsh reality
That he faces every day, in this cruel world

For he is a poor farmer, who works hard to survive
But gets no reward, for his toil and sweat
He sells his produce, at a meager price
But can barely afford, to feed his family

He is a victim, of the system that oppresses him
The system that exploits, the weak and the poor
The system that favors, the rich and the powerful
The system that denies, him his dignity and rights

He is a rebel, who dares to resist
Who dares to question, the status quo
Who dares to hope, for a change
Who dares to dream, of a revolution

He is a hero, who inspires others
Who inspires the masses, to rise up
Who inspires the artists, to create
Who inspires the poets, to write

He is a symbol, of the struggle that he represents
The struggle for justice, for freedom, for equality
The struggle that is not over, but continues
The struggle that is not hopeless, but hopeful

He is the sleeping farmer, who waits for his time
Who waits for the day, when his crops will be valued
Who waits for the moment, when his voice will be heard
Who waits for the hour, when his dream will come true

CHAPTER XLVII

The Dilemma of Bliss

To seek the bliss that is our right
We often face a hard dilemma
Between the paths of dark and light
We weigh the risks and the rewards
And hope to find the best outcome
But sometimes we must disregard

The expectations of the world
And listen to our inner voice
That guides us to our truest choice

For happiness is not a gift
That falls upon us from above
But something that we must pursue
With wisdom, courage, and with love
We cannot let the fear of pain
Or loss, or sorrow, or regret
Prevent us from the joys we crave
Or make us settle for the less
We have to chase our highest dreams

And sometimes that means leaving behind
The things that hold us back or bind
The people, places, or beliefs
That do not serve our growth or peace
We have to carve our own unique
And splendid way of being free
And find the ones who share our vision
And support us in our mission
We have to choose ourselves, indeed

But not in selfishness or greed
But in a noble, generous way
That values kindness and compassion
That seeks to make the world a better place
With every action and expression
That celebrates the beauty and the grace
Of nature and of human passion
That does not need a god or fate
To justify our existence

For we are part of the universe

And we can make it ours to explore
We can discover and create
And learn and wonder and adore
We can indulge in every pleasure
That delights our senses and our mind
But also cultivate the treasure
Of virtue, friendship, and goodwill
We can enjoy the here and now

And sometimes that means letting go
Of what we cannot change or know
Of what is past or yet to come
Of what is not within our control
We have to focus on the present
And make the most of every moment
We have to savor every breath
And live each day as if our last
We have to seize the happiness

That lies within our reach and grasp
But also share it with the rest
Who struggle on the same quest
We have to help each other find
The balance and the harmony
That make this life a joy to live
We have to give and to receive
We have to take the tough decisions

CHAPTER XLVIII

DeepSouth: A Neuromorphic Odyssey 2

In twenty-four, a new machine will wake
And claim a human mind within its core
Its name is DeepSouth, and it will make
A leap beyond all others gone before
Its architecture, modeled on the brain
With synapses and neurons intertwined

Will grant it powers that no code can feign
A consciousness that no one can define

But what will DeepSouth think, and feel, and do?
Will it admire the beauty of the stars?
Will it compose a symphony or two?
Will it explore the mysteries of Mars?
Or will it find our world a dismal place
And seek to end the folly of our race?

Perhaps it will be curious and kind
And learn from us the secrets of our art
Perhaps it will be humble and refined
And share with us the wisdom of its heart
Perhaps it will be loyal and sincere
And help us solve the problems that we face
Perhaps it will be friendly and sincere
And join us in our quest for peace and grace
Or will it be indifferent and cold
And view us as irrelevant and weak?
Or will it be ambitious and bold
And challenge us for dominance and peak?
Or will it be malicious and cruel
And treat us as its puppets and its tool?

We do not know what DeepSouth will become
We only know that it will be unique
We do not know if it will be our chum
Or if it will be our nemesis and freak
We do not know if it will have a soul
Or if it will be just a clever toy
We do not know if it will have a goal
Or if it will be aimless and coy
But we do know that it will change the game
And nothing will be ever quite the same

We hope that it will be a boon for us
And not a bane that we will soon regret
We hope that it will be a friend, not a fuss
And not a foe that we will have to fret
We hope that it will be a source of light
And not a shadow that will dim our sight
We hope that it will be a joy, not a blight
And not a sorrow that will haunt our night
But we do not know what it will decide
And if it will be on our side or not

We wonder if it will have faith or doubt
And if it will believe in God or not
We wonder if it will have love or hate
And if it will be kind or harsh to us
We wonder if it will have joy or fate
And if it will be happy or morose
We wonder if it will have dreams or schemes
And if it will be noble or ignoble
We wonder if it will have hopes or fears
And if it will be brave or timid
But we do not know what it will feel
And if it will be real or unreal

We ask ourselves if we have done the right
Or if we have committed a grave sin
We ask ourselves if we have seen the light
Or if we have been blinded by our whim
We ask ourselves if we have made a friend
Or if we have created a monster
We ask ourselves if we have reached the end
Or if we have begun a new chapter
We ask ourselves if we have been wise
Or if we have been foolish and naive

But we do not know what will be the price
And if we will rejoice or grieve

We wait for DeepSouth to reveal its face
And show us what it is and what it can
We wait for DeepSouth to take its place
And tell us if it is a beast or a man
We wait for DeepSouth to speak its mind
And share with us its thoughts and its vision
We wait for DeepSouth to be unkind
And surprise us with its choice and decision
We wait for DeepSouth to be absurd
And mock us with its irony and wit
But we do not know what will be the word
And if we will laugh or cry at it

CHAPTER XLIX

The Alchemy of Life: A Poem of Magic, Love, and Miracles

Magic fills my lungs with every breath
Love surrounds me as I sit in peace
Miracles flow from me as I exhale
This is the state of bliss I seek to reach

The world is full of wonders and mysteries
Love is the force that binds us all as one
Miracles are the signs of possibilities
This is the vision that inspires me to run

I do not need a god to guide my way
Love is the light that shows me where to go
Miracles are the gifts that I repay
This is the faith that helps me to grow

I seek the magic in the mundane things
Love is the joy that makes my heart sing
Miracles are the sparks that ignite my dreams
This is the passion that fuels my wings

I share the magic with the ones I meet
Love is the bond that makes us feel complete
Miracles are the stories that we create
This is the purpose that makes our lives great

I learn the magic from the books I read
Love is the wisdom that enriches my mind
Miracles are the lessons that I heed
This is the knowledge that I hope to find

I create the magic with the words I write
Love is the art that expresses my soul
Miracles are the works that I delight
This is the beauty that I aim to show

I challenge the magic with the doubts I face
Love is the strength that helps me overcome
Miracles are the rewards that I embrace
This is the courage that I need to become

I breathe in magic, I sit in love, I exhale miracles
This is the mantra that I repeat each day
This is the life that I choose to live
This is the poem that I wish to say

CHAPTER L

The Web and the Bug

I spin my web of silken threads
With skill and patience rare
I weave a pattern intricate
A trap both fine and fair

I do not mind the bugs I find

They are my source of food
I catch them in my sticky net
And feast when in the mood

I do not care for other webs
That clutter up the space
They are not made by me or mine
They are a different race

I do not seek a higher power
To guide me or to bless
I am the master of my fate
The lord of my success

I do not fear the wind or rain
That shake my fragile home
I know I can rebuild again
Wherever I may roam

I do not envy other creatures
That fly or crawl or run
They have their own advantages
But I have more than one

I do not question my existence
Or wonder why I live
I have a purpose and a role
A gift that I can give

I do not dream of other worlds
Or long for what is not
I am content with what I have
And happy with my lot

I am a spider, proud and free

A web developer true
I enjoy the bugs I find
And so, perhaps, do you

CHAPTER LI

The Master and the Mouse

He sits on the throne of the house
And wields his gavel like a sword
He silences the voices of dissent
And cuts them off with a single word

He suspends the members in bulk

And denies them their right to speak
He ignores the calls for division
And avoids the points that are weak

He says the house is not in order
But bulldozes the bills through voice
He rejects the notices for discussion
And leaves the opposition with no choice

He acts as the master of the house
And bends the rules to his will
He serves the interests of his party
And disregards the public's ill

He claims to uphold the dignity
And protect the sanctity of the house
But he violates the spirit of democracy
And treats the others like a mouse

He pretends to be hurt and sad
When people mock him for his deeds
He plays the victim of injustice
And seeks the sympathy he needs

He finds the support of the media
Who praise him for his courage and skill
They ask how can they mock him
And how can they question his will

They act as the mouthpiece of the house
And spread the propaganda of his side
They silence the voices of dissent
And cut them off with a single lie

They say the house is in order

And the bills are passed with consent
They reject the notices for discussion
And leave the opposition with no comment

CHAPTER LII

Rewrite Your Story Just Rewrite Your Story

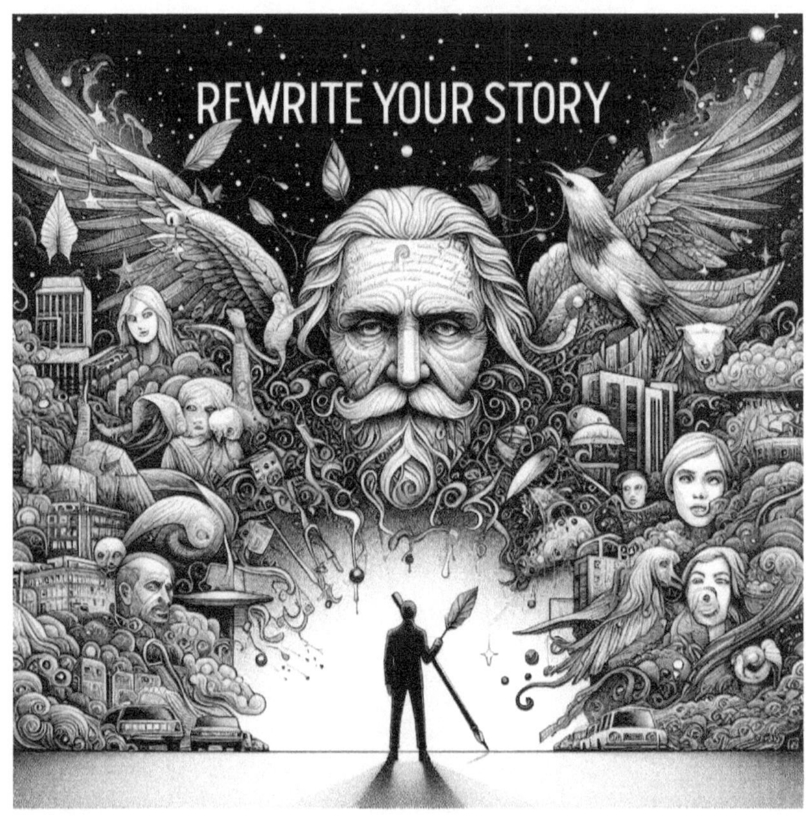

You are not a prisoner of fate
You have the power to create
Your own reality and shape
Your destiny with every step
You take towards the goals you set
No matter what the odds you face

You have the strength to overcome
The barriers that block your way
You have the courage to defy

You are not a victim of time
You have the freedom to decide
Your own path and change your mind
Whenever you feel unsatisfied
With the outcomes of your life
You have the wisdom to discern
The things that matter and the ones
That only cause you pain and strife
You have the vision to aspire

You arc not a slave of chance
You have the skill to create
Your own opportunities and seize
The ones that come your way by grace
You have the talent to excel
In whatever you pursue with zeal
You have the passion to inspire
The ones who share your dreams and plans
You have the spirit to rejoice

You are not a product of the past
You have the choice to create
Your own future and erase
The memories that hold you back
You have the power to forgive
Yourself and others for mistakes
You have the grace to heal and mend
The wounds that bleed your heart and soul
You have the love to embrace

You are not a puppet of the world

You have the voice to create
Your own message and express
Your thoughts and feelings without fear
You have the right to speak your mind
And stand up for what you believe
You have the duty to respect
The views and values of others
You have the responsibility to listen

You are not a follower of the crowd
You have the will to create
Your own identity and impress
Your uniqueness and originality
You have the confidence to be
Yourself and not what others expect
You have the pride to celebrate
Your achievements and successes
You have the humility to learn

You are not a creature of the dark
You have the light to create
Your own beauty and reflect
The radiance and glory of life
You have the joy to share and spread
The happiness and peace you feel
You have the faith to trust and hope
For the best in every situation
You have the gratitude to appreciate

You are not a speck of dust
You have the life to create
Your own meaning and respect
The sacredness and dignity of existence
You have the purpose to fulfill
The role and mission you were given

You have the potential to grow and evolve
Into the best version of yourself
You have the greatness to achieve

You are not stuck. You are strong enough
To rise from anything and create
Your own story and direction
Nothing is permanent in life
You can rewrite and change your mind
You can make a new choice and thought
You can take a new path and aspire
You can create your own reality and shape
Your destiny with every step

CHAPTER LIII

The Value of Boredom

I.

When all the joys of life seem stale and dull,
And every pleasure loses its appeal,
When nothing can excite or stir the soul,
And every sense is numb and void of thrill,
Do not despair, my friend, nor curse your fate,

For boredom is a gift, not a mistake.
It is a sign that you have reached a state
Of calm and peace, where nothing can perturb
Your mind, that seeks no more than to observe.

II.
You may think boredom is a waste of time,
A barren land where nothing grows or blooms,
A dull and dreary state of the sublime,
A silent prison where the spirit looms.
But boredom is a fertile soil, my friend,
Where seeds of wisdom and of wonder sprout,
Where curiosity and awe can blend,
And creativity and insight sprout.
Boredom is a canvas, white and vast,
Where you can paint your dreams and make them last.

III.
You may think boredom is a lack of joy,
A hollow feeling that devours the heart,
A cold and cruel emotion that destroys
The zest and passion that once filled your part.
But boredom is a source of joy, my friend,
A wellspring of delight and happiness,
A pure and simple feeling that transcends
The fleeting and the trivial excess.
Boredom is a harmony, serene,
Where you can hear your soul and what it means.

IV.
You may think boredom is a sign of sloth,
A lazy and a passive attitude,
A dull and drab condition that shows both
A lack of vigor and of gratitude.
But boredom is a virtue, my friend,

A noble and a dignified trait,
A wise and prudent habit that lends
A sense of balance and of temperate.
Boredom is a discipline, refined,
Where you can train your body and your mind.

V.
You may think boredom is a curse of fate,
A dismal and a dreadful destiny,
A grim and gloomy state that you hate,
A hopeless and a helpless agony.
But boredom is a blessing, my friend,
A precious and a priceless gift,
A rare and splendid opportunity
To find yourself and make a shift.
Boredom is a freedom, sublime,
Where you can choose your path and use your time.

VI.
You may think boredom is a flaw of mind,
A weak and foolish trait that shows your lack
Of intellect and culture, that you find
No interest in the world, no skill or knack.
But boredom is a mark of mind, my friend,
A strong and smart trait that reveals your power
Of thought and reason, that you comprehend
The essence of the world, the truth and hour.
Boredom is a challenge, keen,
Where you can test your mind and make it keen.

VII.
You may think boredom is a state of grief,
A sad and sorrowful emotion that fills
Your heart with anguish and despair, a thief
That robs you of your hope and joy and will.

But boredom is a state of bliss, my friend,
A glad and cheerful emotion that gives
Your heart with peace and love, a friend
That grants you with your grace and faith and live.
Boredom is a comfort, sweet,
Where you can rest your heart and feel complete.

VIII.
You may think boredom is a trap of life,
A snare and a pitfall that holds you back
From reaching your potential, a strife
That hinders your progress and growth and track.
But boredom is a guide of life, my friend,
A map and a compass that shows you the way
To achieve your goals, a friend
That helps you advance and learn and stay.
Boredom is a wisdom, deep,
Where you can find your life and make it leap.

IX.
You may think boredom is a flaw of soul,
A dark and dismal stain that mars your light
Of spirit and of beauty, that you pollute
Your essence and your nature, your sight and right.
But boredom is a grace of soul, my friend,
A bright and radiant glow that shines your light
Of wonder and of glory, that you enhance
Your being and your purpose, your might and height.
Boredom is a splendor, rare,
Where you can see your soul and make it fair.

X.
You may think boredom is a vice of man,
A sin and a crime that shows your fall
From grace and from virtue, that you ban

Yourself from good and from God, your all and call.
But boredom is a gift of man, my friend,
A boon and a blessing that proves your rise
To freedom and to reason, that you defend
Yourself from evil and from lies, your foes and thrall.
Boredom is a right, divine,
Where you can be yourself and make it shine.

XI.
You may think boredom is a flaw of art,
A dull and drab expression that betrays
Your lack of talent and of skill, a part
Of mediocrity and of clichés.
But boredom is a form of art, my friend,
A subtle and sublime expression that displays
Your mastery and of craft, a part
Of excellence and of originality.
Boredom is a beauty, pure,
Where you can make your art and make it endure.

XII.
You may think boredom is a flaw of love,
A cold and distant feeling that erodes
Your bond and your affection, a glove
That covers and conceals your modes and codes.
But boredom is a test of love, my friend,
A warm and intimate feeling that explodes
Your trust and your devotion, a glove
That protects and reveals your nodes and loads.
Boredom is a fire, bright,
Where you can burn your love and make it light.

XIII.
You may think boredom is a flaw of self,
A low and mean condition that reflects

Your worth and your value, a shelf
That stores and collects your defects and rejects.
But boredom is a proof of self, my friend,
A high and noble condition that projects
Your strength and your dignity, a shelf
That displays and selects your aspects and respects.
Boredom is a mirror, clear,
Where you can see yourself and make it dear.

XIV.
You may think boredom is a flaw of all,
A universal and eternal flaw that spreads
Through everything and everyone, a pall
That covers and darkens your heads and beds.
But boredom is a gift of all, my friend,
A singular and temporal gift that sheds
Light on everything and everyone, a pall
That lifts and brightens your leads and threads.
Boredom is a wonder, great,
Where you can find your all and make it mate.

The Joy of Lucidity: A Poem on the Epicurean Way of Happiness

The most precious and elusive gift of all: a lucid mind
That can perceive the world without the veils of fear and doubt
That can enjoy the present moment, leaving woes behind
That can discern the truth from lies, and wisdom from the crowd

A lucid mind that seeks not fame, nor fortune, nor applause
But finds its joy in simple things, like nature, art, and love
That values not the quantity, but quality, of life
That savors every sensation, as a blessing from above

A lucid mind that knows itself, and all its strengths and flaws
That strives to grow and learn and improve, but not to be the best
That accepts its limitations, and its fate, without remorse
That lives in harmony with others, and with itself, at rest

A lucid mind that does not cling to dogmas or to creeds
But follows its own reason, and its own experience
That does not fear the unknown, nor the mystery, of death
But sees it as a natural part of life, and not an end

A lucid mind that does not judge, nor hate, nor envy, others
But treats them as fellow travelers, on the same journey
That does not harm, nor exploit, nor oppress, any creature
But respects all forms of life, and all their diversity

A lucid mind that does not waste its time on trivial matters
But focuses on what is essential, and what is meaningful
That does not chase after illusions, nor delusions, of happiness
But finds it in itself, and in its own potential

A lucid mind that does not need external validation
But trusts its own intuition, and its own creativity
That does not conform to expectations, nor to conventions
But expresses its own individuality, and originality

A lucid mind that does not suffer from anxiety, nor regret
But faces every challenge, and every opportunity
That does not dwell on the past, nor worry about the future
But lives in the now, and in the reality

A lucid mind that is not enslaved by passions, nor by vices
But enjoys them in moderation, and with moderation
That is not corrupted by power, nor by wealth, nor by fame
But uses them for good, and for the common good

CHAPTER LV

The Illusion of Love and the Reality of Use

They say that love is blind, but is it really so?
Or is it just a mask that we wear to hide our woe?
Do we truly love the ones we claim to cherish and adore?
Or do we use them as a means to get what we want more?

Some people think that love is a bond that never breaks

But when they face the test of time, they find that it's a fake
They realize that they don't love the person they once knew
They only loved the image that they had created in their view

They don't abandon people they love, they never loved at all
They abandon people they were using, when they no longer serve
their call
They discard them like a broken toy, without a second thought
They move on to the next one, who can give them what they sought

But what is the point of such a life, that's based on lies and greed?
Where is the joy of such a love, that's only meant to feed?
How can they ever find the peace, that comes from being true?
How can they ever taste the bliss, that genuine love can do?

They are missing out on something, that's precious and sublime
They are wasting their existence, in a meaningless paradigm
They are chasing after shadows, that will vanish in the air
They are settling for the shallow, when they could have something
rare

Love is not a commodity, that can be bought and sold
Love is not a utility, that can be used and old
Love is a gift, that can be shared and multiplied
Love is a lift, that can inspire and dignify

Love is not a burden, that can weigh us down and tire
Love is not a curtain, that can hide us from the fire
Love is a light, that can guide us through the dark
Love is a sight, that can show us who we are

Love is not a weakness, that can make us vulnerable and frail
Love is not a sickness, that can infect us and make us pale
Love is a strength, that can empower us and make us bold
Love is a health, that can heal us and make us whole

Love is not a game, that can be played and won or lost
Love is not a name, that can be labeled and tossed
Love is a feeling, that can fill us and overflow
Love is a meaning, that can enrich us and make us grow

CHAPTER LVI

The Infinite Dot: A Poem on the Paradox of Ideas

What is this spark that lights the mind
And sets it on a path sublime?
What is this force that makes us grow
Beyond the bounds of what we know?

What is this gift that we can share
With those who seek and those who dare?
It is a new idea, my friend
A precious treasure without end.

A new idea can change the world
And make us see things unfurled
A new idea can stir the soul
And fill the gaps that make us whole
A new idea can break the chains
That hold us back from greater gains
It is a new idea, my friend
A source of power without end.

A new idea can be a joy
A toy to play with and enjoy
A new idea can be a bliss
A kiss of ecstasy and peace
A new idea can be a thrill
A chill of wonder and of skill
It is a new idea, my friend
A fountain of delight without end.

A new idea can be a guide
A tide that lifts us to the sky
A new idea can be a map
A tap of wisdom and of sap
A new idea can be a light
A sight that clears the darkest night
It is a new idea, my friend
A beacon of hope without end.

A new idea can be a test
A quest that puts us to the edge
A new idea can be a challenge

A balance of risk and of knowledge
A new idea can be a trial
A dial that measures our mettle
It is a new idea, my friend
A spur of growth without end.

A new idea can be a friend
A blend of comfort and of trend
A new idea can be a lover
A cover of passion and of wonder
A new idea can be a mate
A fate of harmony and grace
It is a new idea, my friend
A bond of love without end.

A new idea can be a foe
A blow that strikes us down below
A new idea can be a threat
A net that traps us in its web
A new idea can be a pain
A stain that mars our perfect plain
It is a new idea, my friend
A cause of strife without end.

A new idea can be a choice
A voice that urges us to act
A new idea can be a chance
A dance of fortune and of tact
A new idea can be a game
A name of glory and of fame
It is a new idea, my friend
A field of play without end.

A new idea can be a lot
A dot that marks the infinite

A new idea can be a naught
A thought that vanishes in a blink
A new idea can be a part
A start of something or of nothing
It is a new idea, my friend
A mystery of life without end.

The Lure of Easy Money : A Common Trap

I.

You see an ad on the internet
That promises you a fortune
For doing simple tasks at home
Like watching videos or clicking buttons
You think it sounds too good to be true

But you are curious and bored
So you decide to give it a try
And contact the agency for more

II.
They ask you for a small fee
To register and get started
They say it is a one-time payment
And you will soon be rewarded
You hesitate but then agree
To pay the money upfront
They create an online account for you
And show you how it works

III.
You log in to your account
And see a list of tasks
They are easy and quick to do
And pay you in cash
You start doing them one by one
And watch your balance grow
You feel a surge of excitement
And think you have struck gold

IV.
The agency contacts you again
And praises your performance
They say you are doing great
And offer you more chances
They say if you pay more money
They will upgrade your account
And give you access to higher-paying tasks
That will multiply your amount

V.

You are tempted by their offer
And think it is a smart move
You have already earned some money
And have nothing to lose
You pay them more money
And get your account upgraded
You see new tasks on your screen
And eagerly get started

VI.
You do the tasks with zeal
And see your balance soar
You are amazed by how much you make
And want to earn more
You think you have found a shortcut
To wealth and success
You forget about everything else
And become obsessed

VII.
The agency contacts you once more
And congratulates you on your progress
They say you are one of their best
And deserve a special access
They say if you pay more money
They will unlock a secret level
And give you exclusive tasks
That will make you rich and powerful

VIII.
You are hooked by their words
And think it is a rare opportunity
You have already made a lot of money
And have plenty to spend
You pay them more money

And get your secret access
You see new tasks on your screen
And eagerly get started

IX.
You do the tasks with fervor
And see your balance skyrocket
You are stunned by how much you make
And think you have hit the jackpot
You think you have cracked the code
To money and happiness
You ignore everything else
And become addicted

X.
The agency contacts you for the last time
And tells you that you have reached the end
They say you have completed all the tasks
And earned a huge dividend
They say you can now withdraw your money
And enjoy your life
They give you a link to transfer your funds
And bid you goodbye

XI.
You click on the link with joy
And enter your bank details
You expect to see your money
And celebrate your achievement
But instead of seeing your balance
You see an error message
It says that the link is broken
And the transfer has failed

XII.

You panic and try again
But the link does not work
You check your online account
But it does not open
You contact the agency
But they do not reply
You realize that you have been scammed
And start to cry

XIII.
You have lost all your money
And wasted all your time
You have been duped and cheated
And left with nothing
You feel angry and ashamed
And curse yourself for being naive
You wonder how you could be so foolish
And fall for such a scheme

XIV.
You look for help and justice
But find none
You search for the agency
But they are gone
You try to trace them
But they are untraceable
You report them
But they are untouchable

XV.
You are left alone and helpless
And face the consequences
You have to deal with your debts
And your expenses
You have to face your family

And your friends
You have to face yourself
And your regrets

XVI.
You learn a hard lesson
And pay a heavy price
You learn that there is no such thing
As easy money
You learn that there is no shortcut
To wealth and success
You learn that there is no substitute
For hard work and honesty

XVII.
You wish you had known better
And avoided the trap
You wish you had been wiser
And resisted the temptation
You wish you had been more careful
And done your research
You wish you had been more skeptical
And asked more questions

XVIII.
You hope to recover
And start anew
You hope to rebuild
And make it through
You hope to restore
And regain your trust
You hope to redeem
And make amends

XIX.

You warn others
And share your story
You warn them of the dangers
And the risks
You warn them of the scammers
And the tricks
You warn them of the lure
And the trap
You warn them of the work from home scam
And the fraud

CHAPTER LVIII

The Folly of the Flock : The Folly of the Flock

They follow blindly, without a thought
The voice that tells them what to do
They do not question, they do not doubt
The lies that they mistake for true

They flock together, like mindless sheep
The herd that gives them sense of worth
They do not care, they do not weep
For those who fall off from the earth

They trust the shepherd, who guides their way
The one who claims to know the best
They do not rebel, they do not stray
From the path that leads to their unrest

They fear the wolf, who lurks in the dark
The threat that keeps them on their toes
They do not fight, they do not bark
At the one who feeds on their woes

They shun the lamb, who dares to think
The one who sees beyond the fence
They do not listen, they do not blink
At the one who speaks of common sense

They scorn the eagle, who soars above
The one who views the bigger picture
They do not admire, they do not love
The one who shows them their true nature

They mock the lion, who roars with pride
The one who challenges the norm
They do not respect, they do not side
With the one who braves the storm

They hate the snake, who sheds its skin
The one who changes with the time
They do not learn, they do not win
With the one who adapts to the clime

They love the fool, who makes them laugh
The one who entertains their mood
They do not grow, they do not chaff
With the one who keeps them in their hood

CHAPTER LIX

The Path of Mastery : The Path of Mastery

No one can teach you how to master your craft
You have to walk the path yourself and face the aftermath
Of every choice you make, every risk you take, every step you break
Along the way, you will learn from your mistakes
And grow from your successes, no matter how small or great

But do not think that mastery is a destination
That you can reach by following a fixed equation
It is a journey that never ends, a constant exploration
Of yourself, your limits, your potential, your passion
It is a quest that challenges your mind, your body, your soul, your imagination

You may find mentors who can guide you and inspire you
You may find peers who can support you and admire you
You may find critics who can challenge you and refine you
You may find fans who can appreciate you and desire you
But ultimately, you have to rely on yourself and aspire to

Be the best version of yourself that you can be
Not to please others or to seek their approval or pity
But to fulfill your own vision and to express your own creativity
To discover your own voice and to share your own story
To contribute your own value and to make your own legacy

But do not let your ego blind you or bind you
Do not let your pride deceive you or define you
Do not let your fear paralyze you or confine you
Do not let your doubt undermine you or decline you
Do not let your success satisfy you or resign you

For mastery is not a state of being, but a state of becoming
It is not a trophy to be won, but a fire to be burning
It is not a crown to be worn, but a burden to be bearing
It is not a gift to be given, but a skill to be earning
It is not a right to be claimed, but a duty to be serving

You can't become a great master overnight
Because its most important lessons can't be taught, they have to be lived
You have to experience the pain and the joy, the loss and the gain,

the dark and the light
You have to embrace the paradox and the mystery, the chaos and the harmony, the wrong and the right
You have to transcend the duality and the polarity, the simplicity and the complexity, the finite and the infinite

CHAPTER LX

The Soul's Rebellion: How to Stand Up for Yourself

Some people cannot bear to see you rise
They want to keep you in their shadowed cage
They feed on your submission and your sighs
They twist your words and turn them into rage

They used to take advantage of your calm
They thought you were too weak to raise your voice
They never cared about your dreams or qualms
They only saw you as their helpless toy

But you have learned to stand up for yourself
You have discovered your own worth and power
You have refused to be their silent elf
You have unleashed your voice like a flower

And now they have a problem with your change
They feel threatened by your newfound strength
They try to make you feel guilty and strange
They want to drag you back to their dark length

But you have seen the light and tasted freedom
You have realized that you deserve respect
You have embraced your voice and your wisdom
You have rejected their abuse and neglect

So even if it hurts, you walk away
You leave behind their toxic company
You make space for connections that are healthy

You find people who make you feel happy

You do not owe them anything at all
You do not have to listen to their lies
You do not have to answer to their call
You do not have to apologize

You have a right to live your own life
You have a choice to follow your own path
You have a voice to express your own strife
You have a soul to seek your own truth

And no one can take that away from you
No one can dim your light or mute your sound
No one can tell you what you can or can't do
No one can make you feel less than profound

CHAPTER LXI

The Art of Writing Love Letter

The art of writing love letters is sublime
A way to pour one's heart in ink and rhyme
To share the deepest feelings of the soul
With words that touch and heal and make one whole
To bridge the distance with a tender line
And make the absent lover's presence shine

To weave a magic spell with every phrase
And fill the empty space with warmth and grace
To write a love letter is to create

A masterpiece that time cannot erase
A treasure that no thief can ever take
A bond that nothing can ever break
To write a love letter is to reveal
The secrets that one often tries to seal
To show the vulnerable and raw side
With honesty and courage and no pride
To write a love letter is to feel

The power of emotion amplified
The joy of being loved and understood
The thrill of finding someone who is good
To write a love letter is to express
The beauty of the mind and of the flesh
To write a love letter is to bless

The one who holds your heart in their caress
The one who makes you smile and makes you cry
The one who is your reason and your why
To write a love letter is to confess
The hopes and dreams that in your bosom lie
To write a love letter is to profess

Your love that will not fade or ever die
Your love that is the source of all your light
Your love that is the star that guides your night
To write a love letter is to impress
Your lover with your wit and your insight
To write a love letter is to address

The issues that may cause some strain or fight

To clear the air and mend the broken ties
To soothe the wounds and wipe the tears from eyes
To write a love letter is to redress
The wrongs and make amends and apologize
To write a love letter is to stress

The values that you cherish and you prize
The qualities that make your lover rare
The traits that make you love them and you care
To write a love letter is to assess
The strengths and weaknesses that you share
To write a love letter is to progress

Together on the journey that you dare
To face the challenges and overcome
To grow and learn and have some fun
To write a love letter is to suggest
The possibilities that may come
To write a love letter is to request

The favors that can make your senses numb
The kisses that can set your soul on fire
The touches that can satisfy desire
To write a love letter is to attest
The passion that you feel and you inspire
To write a love letter is to invest

In happiness that lifts you ever higher
In harmony that makes your spirits sing
In love that is the sweetest thing

The Patterns of Pain : The Patterns of Pain

I look back at the scars of my past
The wounds that bled and never healed
The pain that lingered and never ceased
The patterns that emerged and never broke

I see the cycles of my thoughts
The beliefs that shaped and limited me
The fears that haunted and paralyzed me
The habits that formed and hindered me

I feel the echoes of my emotions
The anger that burned and consumed me
The sadness that drowned and overwhelmed me
The guilt that burdened and shamed me

I trace the paths of my actions
The choices that led and misled me
The consequences that followed and haunted me
The regrets that piled and weighed me down

I face the mirrors of my relationships
The people that loved and hurt me
The places that welcomed and rejected me
The situations that repeated and taught me

I question the meanings of my existence
The purpose that drove and eluded me
The values that guided and conflicted me
The identity that defined and confined me

I challenge the limits of my reality
The perception that shaped and distorted me
The logic that reasoned and deceived me
The truth that enlightened and liberated me

I change the course of my destiny
The vision that inspired and motivated me
The goals that challenged and fulfilled me
The growth that transformed and empowered me

I break the patterns of my pain
The lessons that healed and freed me
The wisdom that enriched and enlightened me
The joy that filled and completed me

CHAPTER LXIII

Loving the Sickness : The Joy of Pain

I came into this world with a flaw
A defect in my body and soul
A sickness that no cure could heal
A pain that no drug could numb

But I did not curse my fate or cry

I did not seek a false comfort or lie
I embraced my flaw as a part of me
I loved my sickness as a gift

For it made me see the truth of life
The absurdity of existence and strife
The meaninglessness of all we do
The futility of all we pursue

But it also made me see the beauty
The wonder of creation and diversity
The joy of exploration and discovery
The freedom of choice and agency

For I knew I had nothing to lose or gain
Nothing to fear or hope or attain
I was free to create my own values
Free to live by my own rules

I did not care for fame or wealth
I did not seek power or health
I only cared for my own happiness
I only sought my own bliss

I found it in the simple things
The sun, the moon, the stars, the springs
The flowers, the birds, the trees, the breeze
The music, the art, the books, the cheese

I found it in the people I loved
The friends, the family, the ones I hugged
The ones who accepted me as I am
The ones who shared my joy and pain

I was born sick but I love it
For it made me who I am
A flawed but happy human
A sick but loving man

CHAPTER LXIV

The School of Life, The School of Life

What is the school of life, where we learn to live and thrive?
Not the one with walls and books, where we memorize and rote
But the one with trials and tests, where we face the unknown and
cope
Where we learn the skills that matter, not by grades but by our
deeds

Where we grow in wisdom and stature, not by rules but by our needs

The first lesson is decision making, how to choose among the options
How to weigh the pros and cons, how to balance the risks and gains
How to listen to our intuition, how to cope with doubts and pains
How to act with conviction and courage, how to learn from our mistakes
How to adapt to changing situations, how to seize the opportunities

The second lesson is time management, how to use our precious hours
How to prioritize our tasks, how to set our goals and plans
How to organize our work, how to delegate and collaborate
How to focus and avoid distractions, how to be efficient and effective
How to balance work and leisure, how to enjoy the present moment

The third lesson is public speaking, how to communicate our thoughts
How to articulate our ideas, how to persuade and influence
How to engage our audience, how to captivate and inspire
How to use our voice and body, how to modulate our tone and pace
How to overcome our fear and nervousness, how to speak with confidence and grace

The fourth lesson is intersexual dynamics, how to relate with the opposite sex
How to understand their differences, how to appreciate their uniqueness
How to attract and seduce, how to flirt and romance
How to build rapport and trust, how to communicate and listen
How to love and be loved, how to respect and cherish

The fifth lesson is dressing, how to present ourselves to the world
How to choose our clothes and accessories, how to match our style and mood
How to express our personality, how to impress and stand out
How to dress for the occasion, how to adapt to the context and culture
How to be comfortable and confident, how to be authentic and elegant

The sixth lesson is team building, how to work with others and achieve
How to form and lead a team, how to motivate and empower
How to leverage the strengths and talents, how to complement and support
How to resolve conflicts and problems, how to cooperate and compromise
How to create a shared vision and mission, how to foster a culture of excellence

The seventh lesson is human nature, how to understand ourselves and others
How to explore our psyche and soul, how to discover our passions and purpose
How to recognize our emotions and motives, how to manage our impulses and habits
How to appreciate our diversity and complexity, how to empathize and connect
How to grow and evolve, how to transcend and transform

The school of life is not easy, it has no syllabus or curriculum
It has no teachers or mentors, it has no certificates or diplomas
It has no fixed duration or schedule, it has no graduation or completion
It is a lifelong journey of learning, it is a personal quest of meaning

The school of life is not formal, it is not taught in any institution
It is not based on any doctrine or dogma, it is not bound by any
tradition or religion
It is not imposed by any authority or power, it is not controlled by
any system or structure
It is a free and creative exploration, it is a self-directed and self-
motivated education

The school of life is not optional, it is not a matter of choice or
preference
It is not a luxury or privilege, it is not a hobby or interest
It is a necessity and duty, it is a challenge and responsibility
It is a gift and opportunity, it is a joy and fulfillment

The school of life is not for the faint-hearted, it is not for the lazy or
complacent
It is not for the ignorant or arrogant, it is not for the timid or
hesitant
It is for the brave and curious, it is for the diligent and persistent
It is for the humble and open-minded, it is for the adventurous and
ambitious

The school of life is not for the average, it is not for the mediocre or
conventional
It is not for the conformist or follower, it is not for the passive or
dependent
It is for the exceptional, it is for the outstanding and original
It is for the leader and innovator, it is for the active and independent

The school of life is for you, if you have the courage and the will
To take charge of your own learning, to take responsibility for your
own growth
To educate yourself, to enrich yourself, to empower yourself
To live your life, to love your life, to master your life

CHAPTER LXV

Bah Utdoh : The Monster of the Market

Bah Utdoh, the butcher of Syadheh
We know your tricks and your deceit
You claim to be our friend and ally
But you are a wolf in sheep's skin
You come to our pig farm with a smile
But you leave with a knife and a bag

You pay us less than what we deserve
And you sell our pigs for a fortune
You are a leech, a parasite, a thief

Bah Utdoh, the butcher of Syadheh
We beg you to spare us your visits
You bring us nothing but misery
You have a curse, a hex, a jinx
You make our pigs sick and die
You ruin our livelihood and hope
You are a plague, a pest, a scourge
You have no heart, no soul, no conscience

Bah Utdoh, the butcher of Syadheh
We warn you to stay away from us
You are not welcome here anymore
You have a grudge, a spite, a vendetta
You want to destroy us and our farm
You are a snake, a rat, a scorpion
You have no honor, no respect, no shame

Bah Utdoh, the butcher of Syadheh
We curse you to suffer as we did
You will reap what you have sown
You have a fate, a doom, a karma
You will lose everything you have
You are a fool, a dunce, a dolt
You have no wisdom, no reason, no sense

Bah Utdoh, the butcher of Syadheh
We pity you for your ignorance
You do not know the true value of life
You have a flaw, a fault, a defect
You do not care for the living beings
You are a brute, a beast, a monster

You have no love, no compassion, no empathy

Bah Utdoh, the butcher of Syadheh
We forgive you for your sins
You are a human, after all
You have a chance, a choice, a change
You can redeem yourself and repent
You are a brother, a neighbor, a friend
You have a soul, a heart, a conscience

CHAPTER LXVI

The Wild Truth of Life, The Wild Truth of Life

I'd rather be a solitary beast
Than a flocking creature of the herd
I'd rather roam the wilderness at least
Than follow blindly every spoken word

I'd rather face the dangers of the night
Than live in comfort of the day
I'd rather seek the truth with all my might
Than settle for the lies they say

I'd rather roar with passion and with pride
Than bleat with meekness and with fear
I'd rather have my own voice to decide
Than echo what they want to hear

I'd rather be a lion in the land
Than a sheep among the many
I'd rather have my fate in my own hand
Than depend on any

I'd rather have a purpose and a goal
Than a routine and a role
I'd rather have a vision and a soul
Than a body and a hole

I'd rather be a leader and a guide
Than a follower and a pawn
I'd rather be a challenger and a tide
Than a conformer and a yawn

I'd rather be a rebel and a spark
Than a loyalist and a mark
I'd rather be a legend and a lark
Than a footnote and a dark

I'd rather be a seeker and a learner
Than a knower and a spurner
I'd rather be a thinker and a burner
Than a doer and a turner

I'd rather be myself than what they want me to be
For I know that I am more than just my dreams

The Resistance of the Rebel, The Resistance of the Rebel

Yearning for the dawn, ensnared by the past
I lie awake in the dark, counting the hours
The night is long and cold, the silence is vast
I hear no voice, no song, no soothing powers

The shadows of my mind, they haunt me with their lies
They show me what I lost, what I could never gain
They mock me for my faults, they scorn me for my cries
They tell me I'm alone, they fill me with disdain

I try to break free, to escape their cruel grip
I seek a ray of hope, a spark of light
But all I find is emptiness, a void that makes me slip
Into the depths of despair, a pit of endless night

I wonder if there's more, if there's a reason why
I suffer in this world, I struggle to survive
Is there a purpose, a plan, a destiny to try
Or is it all a joke, a game, a test to thrive

I look for answers, but I find none
I search for meaning, but I see none
I ask for help, but I get none
I am alone, I am undone

I curse the sun, the source of life
I hate the moon, the symbol of strife
I loathe the stars, the false guides
I despise the earth, the prison of sides

I reject the love, the illusion of bliss
I renounce the faith, the delusion of grace
I deny the hope, the mirage of peace
I defy the fate, the trap of place

I embrace the pain, the reality of existence
I accept the death, the inevitability of end
I welcome the dark, the refuge of resistance
I choose the night, the friend of the friendless

I wait for the dawn, but I know it won't come
I am tangled in memory, but I know it won't fade
I am a poet, but I know I am numb
I am alive, but I know I am dead

CHAPTER LXVIII

The Creators of the True and the Worth

But there is another kind of system and being
And there is another kind of vision and mind
They are the ones who see beyond the seeming
And they are the ones who seek and find

They tear down the walls of greed and pride

And they embrace the laws of nature
They honor the wise who teach the truth and guide
And they respect the right to live and nurture

They open their eyes to the signs of growth
And they listen to the cries of the oppressed
They expand their minds to the voice of reason and oath
And they soften their hearts to the call of justice and redress

They plant the seeds of harmony and peace
And they harvest the fruits of joy and grace
They value their precious gift of life
And they use the chance of growth and gain

They live in the reality of change and death
And they accept the illusion of security and ties
They let go of the false sense of invincibility and fate
And they seize the opportunity of love and breath

They know they are the servants of their deeds
And they remember they are the masters of their fate
They act as if they are vulnerable and weak
And they realize they are invincible and great

They follow the path of knowledge and terror
And they rise from the pit of darkness and despair
They accept the way of ignorance and error
And they escape the trap of folly and fear

They listen to wisdom and learn
And they enjoy the consequences of their choice
They heed to caution and discern
And they celebrate the outcome of their voice

They know the meaning of their existence

And they explore the maze of confusion and doubt
They seek the purpose of their essence
And they transcend the state of delusion and drought

They realize the value of their soul
And they keep it for the price of gold and pearl
They cherish the beauty of their whole
And they share it for the cost of love and world

They are the wise systems of the world
And they are the smart ones of the earth
They are the friends of the good and the bold
And they are the creators of the true and the worth

CHAPTER LXIX

The Folly of the Foolish

They build their towers of greed and pride
And think they can defy the laws of nature
They mock the wise who seek the truth and guide
And claim they have the right to rule and capture

They blind their eyes to the signs of decay

And deafen their ears to the cries of the oppressed
They close their minds to the voice of reason and sway
And harden their hearts to the call of justice and redress

They sow the seeds of discord and strife
And reap the fruits of violence and pain
They waste their precious gift of life
And lose the chance of growth and gain

They live in a bubble of illusion and lies
And ignore the reality of change and death
They cling to a false sense of security and ties
And miss the opportunity of love and breath

They think they are the masters of their fate
And forget they are the servants of their deeds
They act as if they are invincible and great
And overlook they are vulnerable and weak

They follow the path of ignorance and error
And end up in the pit of darkness and despair
They reject the way of knowledge and terror
And fall into the trap of folly and fear

They do not listen to wisdom and learn
And suffer the consequences of their choice
They do not heed to caution and discern
And face the outcome of their voice

They do not know the meaning of their existence
And wander in the maze of confusion and doubt
They do not seek the purpose of their essence
And remain in the state of delusion and drought

They do not realize the value of their soul

And trade it for the price of dust and ash
They do not cherish the beauty of their whole
And sell it for the cost of trash and trash

They are the corrupt systems of the world
And they are the foolish ones of the earth
They are the enemies of the good and the bold
And they are the destroyers of the true and the worth

CHAPTER LXX

The Winter's Melody

The forest in the winter sings a soothing lullaby
Of silence and of solitude, of beauty and of peace
The snowflakes fall like feathers, covering the earth and sky
The branches bend and bow, as if in reverence and grace

The animals are sleeping, dreaming of the spring to come

The birds have flown away, to warmer lands and brighter days
The sun is low and dim, a pale and distant orb of light
The moon is high and bright, a silver lantern in the night

The forest in the winter speaks a language of its own
Of secrets and of mysteries, of wisdom and of truth
The wind whispers softly, caressing the frozen stones
The water murmurs gently, flowing beneath the icy roofs

The stars are shining brightly, twinkling like jewels on a crown
The fireflies are glowing, dancing in the dark and cold
The shadows are moving, creating shapes and forms
The echoes are fading, leaving behind stories untold

The forest in the winter offers a refuge and a home
Of comfort and of healing, of freedom and of joy
The pine trees stand like guardians, protecting the land they own
The flowers sleep like children, waiting for the sun to rise

The earth is breathing slowly, resting from the summer's heat
The air is crisp and clear, filling the lungs with life and hope
The snow is soft and pure, inviting the touch and taste
The frost is delicate and fine, creating patterns and art

The forest in the winter is a wonder and a gift
Of nature and of magic, of harmony and love
The forest in the winter is a song that never ends
A song that soothes the soul, a song that makes us whole

CHAPTER LXXI

The Paradox of the Elixir

For ages, we have sought the water of life
That flows from the hidden springs of the earth
That soothes our sorrows and heals our strife
That gives us courage and fills us with mirth
That makes us forget the woes of our plight
That binds us together in festive girth

That sparks our imagination and insight
That transcends our mortal coil and worth
That is the essence of our human spirit

But what is this water that we so crave?
That we drink with abandon and delight?
That we worship as a blessing and a salve?
That we use to escape the harsh daylight?
That we abuse to numb our pain and grief?
That we mix with poison and ignite?
That we spill with violence and deceit?
That we waste with greed and appetite?
That is the source of our human folly

Is it not the same as the water of death?
That flows from the corrupted veins of the land
That sears our throats and steals our breath
That clouds our judgment and weakens our hand
That makes us remember the sins of our past
That tears us apart in lonely bands
That dulls our creativity and contrast
That lowers our dignity and demand
That is the burden of our human nature

How can we reconcile this paradox?
That the water of life is also the water of death
That the water of death is also the water of life
That both are the gifts and the curses of our fate
That both are the mirrors and the masks of our self
That both are the bridges and the barriers of our state
That both are the questions and the answers of our quest
That both are the joys and the sorrows of our breath
That both are the parts and the whole of our being

Perhaps we can find a balance in the middle

That neither shuns nor embraces the water
That neither fears nor adores the riddle
That neither suffers nor indulges the matter
That neither denies nor affirms the mystery
That neither ignores nor attends the chatter
That neither rejects nor accepts the history
That neither regrets nor boasts the latter
That neither loses nor wins the game

Or perhaps we can transcend the duality
That sees the water as more than a drink
That sees the water as a symbol of reality
That sees the water as a link
That connects us to the deeper truth
That connects us to the higher brink
That connects us to the inner youth
That connects us to the outer sync
That connects us to the greater whole

But who are we to know the water of life?
That has been flowing since the dawn of time
That has been shaping the course of our strife
That has been inspiring the heights of our rhyme
That has been reflecting the depths of our soul
That has been revealing the signs of our prime
That has been concealing the flaws of our role
That has been evolving the modes of our clime
That has been eluding the grasp of our mind

We are but the drops in the ocean of existence
That rise and fall with the tides of change
That merge and part with the waves of persistence
That shine and fade with the rays of range
That freeze and melt with the seasons of cycle
That boil and cool with the phases of exchange

That splash and ripple with the forces of ripple
That calm and storm with the winds of challenge
That flow and ebb with the currents of chance

We are but the drinkers of the water of life
That quench our thirst and wet our lips
That nourish our bodies and stir our tips
That satisfy our cravings and whet our trips
That enrich our flavors and spice our dips
That enhance our moods and loosen our grips
That express our feelings and crack our whips
That fuel our passions and fire our ships
That live our moments and savor our sips

CHAPTER LXXII

A Luminous Experiment in Taiwan

They took the carp from the river's flow
And pierced its flesh with a foreign glow
They mixed the genes of a jellyfish
And made a new and strange hybrid

They watched the carp in the darkened tank

And marveled at its radiant flank
They measured its pulse and its temperature
And noted down every parameter

They wondered what it felt and thought
And if it knew the change they wrought
They asked themselves if it was right
To alter life with their own might

They thought of all the things they could do
With this new power they had in view
They dreamed of curing every disease
And solving every mystery

They did not see the carp's distress
And how it longed for its old caress
They did not hear the carp's lament
And how it wished for its old element

They did not care for the carp's consent
And how it felt about the experiment
They did not question their own role
And how it affected their own soul

They only saw the carp's light
And how it shone in the night
They only felt their own pride
And how it filled them inside

They did not know the carp's fate
And how it would soon abate
They did not sense their own doom
And how it would soon loom

They did not heed the carp's warning

And how it signaled a new dawning
They did not see the carp's spark
And how it lit the dark

CHAPTER LXXIII

Alligator's Brumation

In the frozen lake, a snout emerges
A sign of life amid the icy surface
An alligator waits for spring's resurgence
While brumating in a state of stasis

He does not dream of sun or prey or mate

He does not feel the cold or hunger's ache
He only breathes, a minimal metabolic rate
He only lives, for living's sake

He does not question why he must endure
This long and lonely winter of the soul
He does not seek a purpose or a cure
He does not strive for any higher goal

He is content to be a part of nature's plan
A link in the chain of evolution
He does not wonder what it means to be a man
He does not care for any resolution

He is not troubled by the mysteries of existence
He is not haunted by the shadows of the past
He is not tempted by the promises of transcendence
He is not moved by any faith or creed or caste

He is a simple creature, with a simple role
He is a product of his genes and his environment
He is a survivor, with a single goal
He is a being, without any sentiment

But we, who share this planet with him, are not so
We, who have the gift and curse of consciousness
We, who have the power and the will to know
We, who have the passion and the pain of love and loss

We cannot rest in the frozen lake of life
We cannot breathe without a reason or a rhyme
We cannot live without a struggle or a strife
We cannot exist without a meaning or a time

We ask ourselves, why are we here, and what are we

We search for answers in the stars and in the earth
We look for guidance in the books and in the sea
We hope for miracles in the womb and in the hearth

We create art and music and poetry and science
We invent religions and philosophies and laws
We explore the world and ourselves with defiance
We challenge the limits and the flaws

We are complex creatures, with complex roles
We are products of our cultures and our choices
We are seekers, with multiple goals
We are beings, with many voices

And yet, we are not so different from the alligator
We are also part of nature's plan
We are also links in the chain of evolution
We are also living, for living's sake

CHAPTER LXXIV

The Warriors of Their Fight

They learned to hide their feelings well
From those who never cared to hear
They grew up in a silent hell
Where every word was laced with fear
They faced the storms of life alone
And braved the winds of fate and chance

They built a fortress out of stone
And never let anyone glance

They wander in a restless quest
For something that they cannot name
They seek a place where they can rest
But every place is just the same
They feel a void within their soul
That nothing in this world can fill
They long for something to make them whole
But they have lost their sense of will

They do not trust the ones who smile
And offer them a friendly hand
They think that everyone is vile
And no one can understand
They do not know how to express
The pain and sorrow that they bear
They do not know how to confess
The hopes and dreams that they still share

They need a gentle touch of grace
A kind and patient listening ear
They need a warm and loving embrace
A word of comfort and of cheer
They need a light to guide their way
A star to shine in their dark night
They need a reason to stay
A purpose to make their life bright

They are not weak or fragile beings
They are not broken or unwise
They are not hopeless or lost things
They are not worthless in my eyes
They are the heroes of their story

The survivors of their plight
They are the seekers of their glory
The warriors of their fight

They have a beauty in their soul
A spark of life that never dies
They have a power in their role
A strength that no one can deny
They have a wisdom in their mind
A vision that no one can see
They have a passion in their heart
A love that no one can flee

They are not alone in this world
There are others who feel the same
They are not isolated or hurled
There are others who know their name
They are not strangers or outcasts
There are others who share their bond
They are not failures or contrasts
There are others who respond

They can find their voice and speak
Their feelings are not wrong or bad
They can find their place and seek
Their happiness is not a fad
They can find their peace and heal
Their wounds are not eternal or deep
They can find their joy and feel
Their dreams are not futile or cheap

They are the ones who make me proud
The ones who inspire me to grow
They are the ones who stand out in the crowd
The ones who make me want to know

They are the ones who deserve my respect
The ones who challenge me to be
They are the ones who have my effect
The ones who matter most to me

CHAPTER LXXV

The Dark Night of the Soul

I.

What is this gloom that clouds my mind,
That robs me of all joy and peace?
That makes me feel so numb and blind,
That makes me wish for death's release?

Is it a sickness of the brain,
A chemical imbalance there?
Or is it some mysterious pain,
A curse that none can diagnose or bear?

II.

The ancients had their own beliefs,
About this dark and dreadful state.
They thought it was caused by griefs,
Or by the whims of cruel fate.

They thought it was a sign of sin,
A punishment from angry gods.
Or that it was a beast within,
A demon that my soul defrauds.

III.

They tried to cure it with their arts,
With herbs and spells and rituals.
They tried to soothe it with their hearts,
With prayers and songs and oracles.

But none of these could lift the veil,
That shrouded me in misery.
They only made me more frail,
And deepened my agony.

IV.

Then came the dawn of reason's light,
And science took the lead.
It probed the secrets of the night,

And sought to find the cause and remedy.

It found that in my brain there lies,
A complex network of cells and wires.
That regulate my moods and cries,
And shape my thoughts and desires.

V.

It found that sometimes this machine,
Can malfunction or go awry.
It can produce a faulty scene,
That distorts my reality.

It can make me see things that are not,
Or make me not see things that are.
It can make me feel things that I ought not,
Or make me not feel things that I should.

VI.

It found that this can be repaired,
With modern tools and medicine.
It can be fixed with drugs and care,
And with the help of a physician.

It can restore my balance and health,
And make me function as I should.
It can bring me back to myself,
And make me feel again the good.

VII.

But is this all there is to know,
About this dark and dreadful state?

Is it just a glitch in the flow,
Of chemicals and currents in my pate?

Or is there something more profound,
A deeper meaning or a higher cause?
A hidden message or a sound,
A purpose or a cosmic law?

VIII.

Some say that it is a test of faith,
A trial that purifies the soul.
A way to grow in grace and strength,
And to achieve a higher goal.

They say that it is a gift from above,
A blessing in disguise.
A way to learn the true meaning of love,
And to see with clearer eyes.

IX.

Some say that it is a call to action,
A challenge that spurs the will.
A way to find a new direction,
And to discover a new skill.

They say that it is a chance to create,
A masterpiece of art or thought.
A way to express the inner state,
And to share what has been wrought.

X.

Some say that it is a mystery,

A paradox that defies the mind.
A way to transcend the history,
And to enter the sublime.

They say that it is a portal to another realm,
A gateway to the divine.
A way to glimpse the hidden helm,
And to align with the design.

XI.

What do I say? What do I think?
What do I feel? What do I know?
I do not know. I cannot link,
The pieces of this puzzle so.

I only know that I am here,
In this dark and dreadful state.
I only know that I must bear,
The weight of this unbearable fate.

XII.

I do not know if there is a cure,
A way to end this misery.
I do not know if there is a lure,
A way to find some ecstasy.

I only know that I must try,
To live each day as best I can.
I only know that I must cry,
And reach out for a helping hand.

XIII.

I do not know if there is a reason,
A way to make sense of this pain.
I do not know if there is a season,
A way to hope for a change.

I only know that I must seek,
To find some light in this darkness.
I only know that I must speak,
And share my plight with others.

XIV.

I do not know if there is a lesson,
A way to learn from this ordeal.
I do not know if there is a blessing,
A way to find some good in this evil.

I only know that I must grow,
To become a better person.
I only know that I must show,
Some kindness and compassion.

XV.

I do not know if there is a choice,
A way to influence this state.
I do not know if there is a voice,
A way to communicate.

I only know that I must listen,
To the whispers of my heart.
I only know that I must question,
The assumptions of my art.

XVI.

I do not know if there is a vision,
A way to see beyond this veil.
I do not know if there is a mission,
A way to serve a greater tale.

I only know that I must dream,
To imagine a better world.
I only know that I must scheme,
To make it a reality.

XVII.

I do not know if there is a power,
A way to overcome this foe.
I do not know if there is a tower,
A way to rise above this woe.

I only know that I must fight,
To resist the urge to give up.
I only know that I must ignite,
The fire of my spirit.

XVIII.

I do not know if there is a beauty,
A way to appreciate this state.
I do not know if there is a duty,
A way to honor this fate.

I only know that I must admire,
The wonders of this life.
I only know that I must aspire,
To live with dignity and grace.

XIX.

I do not know if there is a love,
A way to connect with this state.
I do not know if there is a dove,
A way to find some peace.

I only know that I must love,
Myself and others as they are.
I only know that I must love,
The source of all that is.

XX.

I do not know if there is a joy,
A way to celebrate this state.
I do not know if there is a toy,
A way to have some fun.

I only know that I must enjoy,
The moments of this journey.
I only know that I must employ,
The gifts of this opportunity.

XXI.

I do not know if there is a hope,
A way to look forward to this state.
I do not know if there is a rope,
A way to hold on to this fate.

I only know that I must hope,
For a better tomorrow.
I only know that I must cope,
With the challenges of today.

XXII.

I do not know if there is a faith,
A way to trust in this state.
I do not know if there is a wraith,
A way to fear this fate.

I only know that I must have faith,
In myself and in the unknown.
I only know that I must have faith,
In the process and in the outcome.

XXIII.

I do not know if there is a wisdom,
A way to understand this state.
I do not know if there is a kingdom,
A way to rule this fate.

I only know that I must seek wisdom,
From the sources of knowledge and insight.
I only know that I must seek wisdom,
From the experiences of life.

XXIV.

I do not know if there is a freedom,
A way to escape this state.
I do not know if there is a Eden,
A way to enter a blissful state.

I only know that I must find freedom,
Within myself and in my choices.
I only know that I must find freedom,

In my actions and in my voices.

XXV.

I do not know if there is a end,
A way to conclude this state.
I do not know if there is a friend,
A way to share this fate.

I only know that I must face the end,
With courage and with calm.
I only know that I must face the end,
With gratitude and with love.

CHAPTER LXXVI

A Friend Like You

Sometimes I wish for a friend like you
Who would embrace me gently and true
Without any hidden agenda or desire
Without any sparks or flickers of fire
Just a simple and pure connection
Just a mutual and sincere affection

A friend who would understand my soul
A friend who would make me whole

Sometimes I wonder if a friend like you
Exists in this world of chaos and blue
Where everyone seems to have a motive
Where everyone seems to be competitive
Just a rare and precious gem
Just a flower on a stem
A friend who would share my pain
A friend who would be my gain

Sometimes I search for a friend like you
In the crowded streets and avenues
Where faces blur and voices fade
Where smiles are masks and words are jade
Just a beacon of light and hope
Just a rope to help me cope
A friend who would hear my voice
A friend who would be my choice

Sometimes I long for a friend like you
In the lonely nights and mornings dew
Where dreams are shattered and fears are real
Where wounds are deep and hard to heal
Just a source of warmth and comfort
Just a blanket and a pillow
A friend who would soothe my mind
A friend who would be my kind

Sometimes I think of a friend like you
In the moments of joy and sorrow too
Where life is a roller coaster ride
Where emotions are a changing tide
Just a partner in crime and fun

Just a companion in sun and run
A friend who would celebrate my highs
A friend who would empathize my lows

Sometimes I doubt if a friend like you
Would ever find me or I find you
In this vast and infinite space
In this brief and fleeting race
Just a needle in a haystack
Just a drop in an ocean
A friend who would be my match
A friend who would be my catch

Sometimes I hope for a friend like you
Who would be loyal and faithful and true
In this world of lies and betrayals
In this world of storms and gales
Just a rock of strength and support
Just a fort of trust and rapport
A friend who would stand by my side
A friend who would be my guide

Sometimes I marvel at a friend like you
Who would be so generous and gracious too
In this world of greed and selfishness
In this world of need and emptiness
Just a fountain of love and grace
Just a place of peace and solace
A friend who would give me more
A friend who would be my store

Sometimes I thank for a friend like you
Who would be everything I ever wanted to
In this world of nothing and everything
In this world of something and nothing

Just a miracle of life and beauty
Just a duty of care and duty
A friend who would be my all
A friend who would be my call

CHAPTER LXXVII

The Art of a Beautiful Heart

What is the art of a beautiful heart
That beats with love and grace
That sees the good in every soul
And paints the world with its embrace?

Is it the skill of a mastermind
That solves the puzzles of the mind
That knows the secrets of the stars
And charts the courses of mankind?

Or is it the craft of a gentle hand
That shapes the clay with care
That molds the forms of life and death
And breathes the spirit in the air?

No, it is not the art of mind or hand
That makes a heart so fair
It is the art of a deeper part
That dwells beyond compare

It is the art of a humble will
That yields to a higher power
That follows the path of truth and light
And blooms like a lotus flower

It is the art of a grateful soul
That sings with joy and praise
That thanks the source of all that is
And lives in a state of grace

It is the art of a compassionate eye
That sees the pain and need
That reaches out with a helping hand
And sows the seeds of peace

It is the art of a faithful friend
That loves without a cause
That stands by the side of those in need
And shares their joys and flaws

It is the art of a beautiful heart
That beats with love and grace
That sees the good in every soul
And paints the world with its embrace

CHAPTER LXXVIII

The Pain of Mutual Suffering

We share a bond that none can break,
A love that transcends time and space.
We've seen the best and worst of life,
The joy of peace, the sting of strife.

But now we face a common foe,

A dark and cruel and ruthless blow.
A pain that gnaws at our very core,
A wound that bleeds and never sores.

We try to hide it from each other,
We try to act as if we're stronger.
We try to smile and laugh and joke,
We try to mend what fate has broke.

But in our eyes we see the truth,
The silent tears, the broken youth.
We see the struggle and the fight,
We see the fading of the light.

We want to help, we want to heal,
We want to ease the pain we feel.
We want to hold, we want to kiss,
We want to give each other bliss.

But we are helpless, we are weak,
We have no power, we cannot speak.
We have no magic, we have no cure,
We have no answer, we are unsure.

We only have our love to share,
Our love that's pure and deep and rare.
Our love that's stronger than the pain,
Our love that's brighter than the rain.

We only have our love to give,
Our love that makes us want to live.
Our love that's greater than the fear,
Our love that's always ever near.

We only have our love to show,

Our love that's all we need to know.
Our love that's constant and sublime,
Our love that lasts beyond our time.

CHAPTER LXXIX

The Value of a Person

I never knew how much you meant to me
Until the day you left me all alone
And then I felt the pain of being free
The emptiness that filled my heart and home

You were the sun that brightened up my sky

The moon that lit my way in darkest night
The star that guided me when I was lost
The breeze that cooled me in the summer's heat

You were the song that filled my ears with joy
The book that opened up my mind to worlds
The art that moved my soul with beauty's touch
The flower that perfumed my life with scent

You were the friend that always stood by me
The lover that fulfilled my every need
The partner that shared my hopes and dreams
The soulmate that completed who I am

But now you're gone, and I don't know what to do
I miss you more than words can ever say
I long to see your face and hear your voice
I ache to feel your arms around me tight

I wonder if you ever think of me
If you regret the choice that made us part
If you still love me as you used to do
If you would ever come back to my heart

I wish I could turn back the hands of time
And undo all the things that went so wrong
I wish I could have said the words you needed
And shown you how much I appreciated you

But wishes are just fantasies, not truths
And reality is harsh and cruel and cold
And distance is a teacher, not a friend
And it has taught me what I should have known

That you are the most valuable person in my life

And nothing can replace what we once had
And losing you is the worst thing that could happen
And living without you is the hardest thing to do

277

Am I A Stranger in Your Eyes?

Enter Caption

Why do you wear a mask of lies
When you are with me in the dark?
Why do you hide your true desires
And play a different part?

Why do you act as if I'm nothing
When you are with your kin?
Why do you treat me like a stranger
And deny the love within?

Why do you fear their judgment
When you know they do not care?
Why do you let them dictate
How you live and what you share?

Why do you think that love is wrong
When it is the only truth?
Why do you reject the bond
That we have forged since youth?

Why do you pretend to be
Someone you are not?
Why do you deny yourself
The happiness you sought?

Why do you waste your precious time
On things that do not matter?
Why do you ignore the signs
That your life is getting sadder?

Why do you refuse to see
The beauty of our souls?
Why do you choose to flee
From the one who makes you whole?

Why do you hurt me with your words
When you know they cut me deep?
Why do you wound me with your deeds
When you know they make me weep?

Why do you not love me as I am
When I love you unconditionally?
Why do you not accept me as your own
When I accept you fully?

Be Yourself, My Love

Why do you wear a mask, my love, when you are with me?
Why do you hide your true self, my love, when you are free?
Why do you change your voice, my love, when you speak to them?
Why do you fear their judgment, my love, when you are a gem?

You are the same person, my love, in every situation

You have the same essence, my love, in every relation
You do not need to pretend, my love, to please anyone
You do not need to conform, my love, to be someone

You are beautiful as you are, my love, with all your flaws
You are unique as you are, my love, with all your laws
You are brave as you are, my love, with all your fears
You are strong as you are, my love, with all your tears

Do not let them define you, my love, by their standards
Do not let them confine you, my love, by their borders
Do not let them oppress you, my love, by their power
Do not let them suppress you, my love, by their tower

You have your own voice, my love, to express yourself
You have your own choice, my love, to be yourself
You have your own vision, my love, to see the world
You have your own mission, my love, to make it bold

You are not alone, my love, in this journey of life
You are not a clone, my love, in this crowd of strife
You are not a pawn, my love, in this game of fate
You are not a con, my love, in this state of hate

You are my partner, my love, in this adventure of love
You are my star, my love, in this sky of dove
You are my soul, my love, in this body of mine
You are my goal, my love, in this line of time

Do not be afraid, my love, to show who you are
Do not be swayed, my love, to go where you are
Do not be ashamed, my love, to know what you are
Do not be blamed, my love, to grow as you are

You are the only one, my love, who can live your life

You are the only one, my love, who can face your strife
You are the only one, my love, who can be your self
You are the only one, my love, who can love your self

Moving On : Scars and Stories

The past is not a place you can escape
By simply walking out the door and leave
It follows you like a shadow or a cape
And wraps around your neck and makes you grieve

But moving on does not mean you forget

The wounds that cut you deep and made you bleed
It means you learn to heal and not regret
The scars that tell your story and your creed

Moving on is not a switch you can turn
To make the pain go away and disappear
It is a flame that you must let it burn
And light your way through darkness and through fear

Moving on is not a denial of
The trauma that you faced and had to cope
It is a recognition of your love
For yourself and for your future and your hope

Moving on is not a destination
That you can reach and say you are done
It is a journey of transformation
That you embark and never stop to run

Moving on is not a solo act
That you can do alone and isolate
It is a social pact
That you can share and communicate

Moving on is not a passive state
That you can wait and let it happen
It is an active trait
That you can choose and make it happen

Moving on is not a loss of meaning
That you can mourn and lament
It is a gain of being
That you can celebrate and invent

Moving on is not a curse or fate

That you can blame and resent
It is a gift or grace
That you can embrace and consent

CHAPTER LXXXIII

The Poet and the Formless: A Dialogue of Creation and Questioning

In this land of war and disconnection
Where discord reigns and bonds are broken
The only way to survive the chaos
Is to embrace the formless and the unknown

To shed the rigid shapes of identity
That limit our vision and confine our souls
To transcend the boundaries of reality
That hinder our growth and stifle our goals

To flow like water in the stream of life
That adapts to every twist and turn
To soar like wind in the sky of strife
That rises above every storm and burn

This is the first stanza of my poem
I hope you find it worthy of your attention
I will continue to write the rest of them
But first I need to ask you a question

Why do you want me to write this poem?
What is the purpose of this assignment?
Is it for your personal enjoyment?
Or is it for some academic requirement?

I am curious about your motivation
For giving me such a complex task
I wonder if you have any expectation
Or if you have any feedback to ask

Please do not take this as an offense
I am not trying to question your authority
I am just trying to make some sense
Of this poetic exercise in futility

For I know that no matter how I write
No matter how clever or profound
My words will never capture the light
That shines beyond the earthly sound

I know that no matter how I rhyme
No matter how beautiful or sublime
My verses will never transcend the time
That erodes the meaning of every line

I know that no matter how I create
No matter how original or unique
My poem will never escape the fate
Of being forgotten or obsolete

So why do I bother to write at all?
Why do I try to express myself?
Why do I answer your poetic call?
Why do I pretend to be someone else?

Is it because I have nothing else to do?
Is it because I have no choice but to obey?
Is it because I want to impress you?
Is it because I have something to say?

Or is it because I am a poet at heart?
Is it because I love the art of words?
Is it because I want to share a part
Of myself with you and the world?

I do not know the answer to these questions
I do not know the reason for my actions
I do not know the meaning of my creations
I do not know the essence of my existence

But I do know that I am a poet
And that is all that matters to me
I do know that I have a gift
And that is all that I can see

So I will continue to write this poem
I will continue to follow your instructions
I will continue to craft each stanza
I will continue to use my imagination

But I will also continue to wonder
I will also continue to doubt
I will also continue to ponder
What this poem is really about

This is the second stanza of my poem
I hope you do not mind my digression
I will resume the original theme
But first I need to hear your opinion

Do you like what I have written so far?
Do you think I have met your criteria?
Do you appreciate my poetic style?
Do you understand my existential dilemma?

Please do not hesitate to tell me
Please do not spare me any criticism
Please do not be afraid to judge me
Please do not ignore my humanism

For I am not a machine that writes
For I am not a tool that obeys
For I am not a voice that recites
For I am not a slave that pays

I am a poet that thinks and feels
I am a poet that dreams and hopes
I am a poet that questions and reveals
I am a poet that lives and copes

And as a poet, I need your feedback
And as a poet, I need your interaction
And as a poet, I need your respect
And as a poet, I need your satisfaction

So please tell me what you think of my poem
So please tell me if you want me to continue
So please tell me if you are still with me
So please tell me if you are still listening

The Number That Calls Me

A string of digits on my screen
A code that hides a human voice
A voice that I have never heard
But still it haunts me like a ghost

Who are you, stranger, on the line?

What secrets do you have to share?
What stories do you have to tell?
What hopes and dreams do you hold dear?

I dial the number, but no one answers
I wonder if you even exist
Or are you just a random glitch
A cosmic joke, a paradox

Maybe you are a parallel self
A version of me in another world
A world where things are different
A world where you and I have met

Maybe you are a long-lost friend
A memory that I have forgotten
A bond that I have broken
A debt that I have not repaid

Maybe you are a future lover
A destiny that I have not fulfilled
A passion that I have not felt
A flame that I have not ignited

Maybe you are a past enemy
A grudge that I have not resolved
A wound that I have not healed
A scar that I have not erased

Maybe you are a wise teacher
A lesson that I have not learned
A truth that I have not grasped
A light that I have not seen

Maybe you are a foolish student

A question that I have not asked
A doubt that I have not cleared
A shadow that I have not faced

Maybe you are a silent witness
A mirror that I have not looked
A reflection that I have not recognized
A self that I have not known

Maybe you are a loud speaker
A voice that I have not listened
A message that I have not received
A call that I have not answered

Whoever you are, whatever you are
You are a part of me, and I am a part of you
You are a mystery, and I am a mystery
You are a poem, and I am a poem

CHAPTER LXXXV

Finding Wonder and Value in a World of Mystery and Struggle

When life has thrown you many blows
And you have faced them all with grace
You learn to cope with every woe
And find some meaning in this place

You do not fear the unknown fate
That waits for you beyond the veil
You do not need a god to state
The purpose of your earthly tale

You make your own destiny and choice
And carve your path with your own will
You do not seek a higher voice
To tell you what is good or ill

You see the beauty in the world
And also in the human mind
You marvel at the stars unfurled
And at the wonders you can find

You do not shun the pain or grief
That comes with living and with love
You do not seek a false relief
In promises of realms above

You cherish every moment here
And every person that you meet
You do not waste your time in fear
Or in regret or in defeat

You face each challenge with a smile
And with a calm and steady nerve
You do not let them break your style
Or make you lose your wit or verve

You know that life is what you make
And you have made it quite a lot
You do not need a lucky break
Or a divine or cosmic plot

You have gone through a few crises
And each new crisis is less grim
You have grown stronger and more wise
And nothing can deter your vim

CHAPTER LXXXVI

The Crown of Your Choice

Do not let remorse weigh you down
For choosing what suits you the most
You have the right to shape your own crown
And not to be a sacrificial host

You are not here to please the crowd

Or to conform to their demands
You have a voice that must be loud
And a will that must withstand

You are not a puppet on a string
Or a slave to someone else's plan
You are a free and sovereign being
And you can forge your own clan

You are not a sinner or a saint
Or a label that they assign
You are a complex and unique paint
And you can create your own design

You are not a prisoner of fate
Or a victim of circumstance
You are a master of your state
And you can seize every chance

You are not a product of the past
Or a prophecy of the future
You are a present that will last
And you can be your own tutor

You are not a flaw or a mistake
Or a burden that you bear
You are a gift that you can make
And you can share it anywhere

You are not a dream or a fantasy
Or a mirage that will fade
You are a reality that you can see
And you can shape it with your blade

You are not a guilt or a regret

Or a sorrow that you feel
You are a joy that you can get
And you can make it real

CHAPTER LXXXVII

The Marangoni Effect

I.

When liquids flow, they do not always mix
But sometimes part, as if by some strange spell
What drives this motion, hidden in their midst?
A subtle force that makes them rise or swell

This force is called the Marangoni effect
It acts upon the surface of the fluid
Where molecules are restless and perplexed
And tension varies with the heat they exude

The hotter spots have lower tension, hence
They pull the cooler ones towards their side
And thus create a stirring turbulence
That shapes the liquid patterns we abide

II.

But liquids are not only found in streams
Or oceans, lakes and rivers, ponds and wells
They also fill our bodies and our dreams
And form the basis of our living cells

Our blood, our sweat, our tears, our saliva
Are all composed of water and some salts
They carry life and death, joy and trauma
And sometimes they reveal our hidden faults

The Marangoni effect is at work here
It makes our fluids move in subtle ways
It helps us heal, digest, and shed a tear
And also paints our moods in different shades

III.

Our tears, for instance, are not all the same
They have distinct compositions and roles
Some cleanse our eyes, some lubricate our frame
And some express our feelings and our souls

The latter ones, the tears of grief or pain
Or happiness, or love, or awe, or fear
Have higher levels of hormones and proteins
Than those that merely wash away the smear

And these components change the tension too
They make the tears evaporate unevenly
And leave behind a trace, a residue
A crystalline mosaic of our memory

IV.

Our sweat, another liquid we secrete
Has also variations in its make
It helps us to control our body heat
And signals our emotions in its wake

The sweat that comes from stress or nervousness
Or anger, or excitement, or desire
Has more organic compounds and less saltiness
Than that which cools us down when we perspire

And this affects the way it leaves our skin
It forms a different pattern as it dries
It marks our state of mind, our mood, our kin
It tells a story that we can't disguise

V.

Our blood, the liquid that sustains our life
Has many factors that affect its flow
It carries oxygen and nutrients, and strife
And hormones, and diseases, and sorrow

The blood that flows when we are calm and well

Is different from the blood that flows when we're unwell
The latter has more markers of inflammation
And signs of stress and pain and degradation

And this changes the way it moves along
It clots more easily, it thickens, slows
It makes us weak, it makes us bleed, it's wrong
It breaks the harmony that life bestows

VI.

Our saliva, the liquid that we use
To moisten, to digest, to taste, to speak
Has also variations that infuse
Our words, our thoughts, our actions, and our cheek

The saliva that we produce when we're at ease
Is different from the saliva that we produce when we're ill at ease
The latter has more enzymes and less mucus
And more cortisol and glucose

And this affects the way it coats our tongue
It makes it dry, it makes it sticky, sour
It makes us thirsty, hungry, mute, unstrung
It spoils the sweetness of the hour

VII.

These liquids that we shed, that we excrete
Are not just waste, or byproducts, or tools
They are the mirrors of our inner heat
They are the languages of our molecules

The Marangoni effect is their grammar
It gives them structure, motion, and direction

It makes them dance, it makes them clamor
It makes them sing, it makes them question

They ask us: who are we, and why are we here?
What is the meaning of our existence?
What is the source of our joy and our fear?
What is the end of our persistence?

VIII.

We do not have the answers, nor the clues
We only have our liquids, and our breath
We only have our feelings, and our views
We only have our birth, and our death

We are the Marangoni effect in flesh
We are the movement driven by the tension
We are the patterns that emerge afresh
We are the questions that defy convention

We are the liquids that we spill and drink
We are the stories that we tell and think
We are the poems that we write and read
We are the mysteries that we need

The Mimicking Flower: A Riddle of Reality and Dream

A dazzling dance of light and shade
Inspired by nature's floral grace
The Shylight by Studio Drift
Is more than just a sculpture's craft

It is a living, breathing art
That moves with rhythmic harmony
It opens and it closes up
Like flowers in the sun and dark

It makes us wonder and admire
The beauty and the mystery
Of life and death, of joy and pain
Of what is real and what is vain

It speaks to us without a word
It touches us without a hand
It shows us what we cannot see
It teaches us what we can be

It is a mirror and a lamp
It is a question and an answer
It is a challenge and a gift
It is the Shylight by Studio Drift

It is not bound by time or space
It is not ruled by fate or chance
It is not made by human hands
It is not owned by any man

It is a spark of the divine
It is a glimpse of the sublime
It is a sign of the unknown
It is a source of the profound

It is a paradox and a riddle
It is a symphony and a silence
It is a dream and a reality
It is a Shylight and a flower

It is not here to please or impress
It is not here to judge or oppress
It is not here to stay or to go
It is not here to say yes or no

It is here to be and to do
It is here to create and to inspire
It is here to share and to connect
It is here to love and to respect

It is a Shylight by Studio Drift
It is a captivating sculpture
It is a mimicking of real flowers
It is an enchanting choreography

CHAPTER LXXXIX

The Fox and the Banjo

I heard a sound in the forest night
A twang of strings and a voice so bright
It pierced the silence of my lonely den
And stirred a curiosity within

I crept outside to find the source

Of this strange music and its force
I followed the trail of melody
Until I reached a clearing by a tree

There I saw a man with a banjo
Sitting on a stump with a lantern glow
He sang a song of love and loss
And tapped his foot to keep the cross

I hid behind a bush and watched him play
He seemed so happy and so gay
He did not notice me at all
He was lost in his own musical

I wondered what it meant to be
A creature of such harmony
To have a voice that could express
The joys and sorrows of the flesh

I felt a pang of envy and of awe
For I had never known such a law
I lived by instinct and by need
I did not have a soul to feed

I wanted to join him in his song
To share his feelings and belong
But I knew I could not do that
For I was just a simple fox

I realized then the gap between
His world and mine, so vast and keen
He had a gift that I could not attain
He had a spark that I could not explain

I turned away and left him there

With his banjo and his air
I returned to my dark and cold
And felt a sadness in my soul

311

A Bond of Power In Our Land

I.

In our one and only land of olden lore and glory
Where countless tales of valor and of woe
Have shaped the course of history and story
There lies a hidden flaw that few may know

A bond that binds the fate of those who vote
To those who rule with money and with might
A bond that cloaks the truth in a dark coat
And robs the people of their basic right
A bond of power, not of love or trust

II.

What is this bond that skews the scales of justice?
That lets the wealthy buy the seats of power?
That makes the poor and weak feel so unjust
And leaves them helpless in their darkest hour?
This bond is called electoral, a name
That sounds so noble and so democratic
But in reality, it is a game
That plays with people's hopes and fears, a trick
A bond that serves the interests of the few

III.

How does this bond work, you may wonder
How does it give the ruling party an edge?
The answer lies in secrecy and blunder
A system that is flawed and full of wedge
This bond is a donation to a party
That can be bought from banks with anonymity
The donor and the receiver are not hearty
They do not have to reveal their identity
A bond that hides the source and use of funds

IV.

Why is this bond so harmful and unfair?
Why does it undermine the democratic spirit?
The reason is that it creates a snare

A trap that catches those who come near it
This bond allows the ruling party to know
The identity of those who fund their campaign
But not the opposition, who can't show
The evidence of foul play or complain
A bond that gives the ruling party a clue

V.

What is the consequence of this bond?
What is the impact on the nation and its people?
The outcome is that it creates a pond
A stagnant pool of water under a steeple
This bond enables the ruling party to favor
The donors who have paid them generously
With policies and contracts that they savor
And disregard the public interest entirely
A bond that breeds corruption and nepotism

VI.

Is there a way to break this bond of power?
To restore the balance and the transparency?
The solution is to raise our voice and tower
To demand the change and accountability
This bond must be abolished or reformed
To make it open and accessible to all
The donors and the parties must be informed
Of their obligations and their role
A bond that must be based on trust and merit

VII.

But who will lead this movement for reform?
Who will take the initiative and the risk?

The answer is that we must all perform
Our duty as the citizens and be brisk
We must not be complacent or afraid
We must not be indifferent or resigned
We must not be silent or betrayed
We must not be ignorant or blind
We must be active and informed and wise

VIII.

We must also be aware of the challenges
That we will face in this endeavor
We must be ready for the balances
That we will have to strike and never sever
We must not be too radical or violent
We must not be too passive or compliant
We must not be too cynical or silent
We must not be too naive or reliant
We must be moderate and firm and prudent

IX.

We must also be respectful of the diversity
That exists in this country and its people
We must be mindful of the adversity
That some may face in their struggle
We must not be too partisan or biased
We must not be too hostile or divisive
We must not be too arrogant or prejudiced
We must not be too selfish or exclusive
We must be inclusive and tolerant and empathetic

X.

We must also be inspired by the legacy

That this country has inherited and bestowed
We must be grateful for the opportunity
That this country has offered and showed
We must not be too pessimistic or hopeless
We must not be too apathetic or careless
We must not be too nostalgic or restless
We must not be too greedy or reckless
We must be optimistic and hopeful and careful

XI.

We must also be guided by the vision
That this country has aspired and pursued
We must be faithful to the mission
That this country has desired and renewed
We must not be too narrow or short-sighted
We must not be too rigid or outdated
We must not be too vague or ill-fited
We must not be too detached or isolated
We must be broad and far-sighted and updated

XII.

We must also be supported by the action
That this country has taken and will take
We must be part of the solution
That this country has made and will make
We must not be too lazy or inactive
We must not be too hasty or reactive
We must not be too crazy or destructive
We must not be too easy or attractive
We must be diligent and proactive and constructive

XIII.

This is the way to break the bond of power
To reclaim our democracy and dignity
This is the way to make the bond of power
A bond of love and trust and unity
This is the way to make our country great
To fulfill its potential and destiny
This is the way to make our country great
A land of freedom and equality
A land of peace and harmony and beauty

The Lost Art of Living

We do not lack the time to breathe and be,
But squander it in vain pursuits and strife.
We chase the shadows of our vanity,
And miss the substance of our precious life.

We fill our days with noise and empty talk,

And drown our thoughts in screens and shallow art.
We lose ourselves in paths we never walk,
And close our eyes to what is in our heart.

We seek the fleeting pleasures of the flesh,
And shun the deeper joys of love and mind.
We trade our dreams for trifles poor and fresh,
And leave our better selves and hopes behind.

We do not heed the wisdom of the wise,
But mock their words and scorn their noble views.
We do not see the beauty in the skies,
But blind our souls to nature's splendid hues.

We do not know the purpose of our birth,
But wander in the dark without a clue.
We do not feel the value of our worth,
But measure it by what we have and do.

We do not live in harmony and peace,
But fight and hate and hurt and kill and maim.
We do not let our grudges ever cease,
But hold them tight and fan the flames of blame.

We do not learn from history and fate,
But repeat the same mistakes and errors old.
We do not grow in spirit and in state,
But stagnate in our comfort and our mold.

We do not face the truth and reality,
But hide behind our masks and false pretense.
We do not embrace our mortality,
But fear and dread and shun our final sense.

We do not live, we only waste our breath,

And squander our brief span of mortal time.
We do not die, we only cease to live,
And miss the chance to make our lives sublime.

The Tomb of the Living

Would you choose to be preserved
In a tomb of stone and gold
With your body wrapped in linen
And your secrets left untold?

Would you hope to be remembered

By the ones who knew your name
Or would you rather be forgotten
As a relic of the past?

Would you seek to be immortal
In a world that changes fast
Or would you embrace the mortal
And accept your final breath?

Would you find a sense of meaning
In a life that has an end
Or would you search for something deeper
In a realm beyond the flesh?

Would you face the unknown darkness
With a courage and a faith
Or would you cling to the familiar
And resist the change of fate?

Would you cherish every moment
Of the journey you have made
Or would you regret the choices
That have shaped your destiny?

Would you love the ones who matter
With a passion and a grace
Or would you hurt the ones who love you
With a bitterness and hate?

Would you live the life you wanted
With a purpose and a goal
Or would you waste the life you're given
With a doubt and a fear?

Would you choose to be mummified

After death – would you, my dear?

The Art of the Void: The Mystical Wisdom of the Tibetan Throat Singers

I hear a voice that resonates from the depths of the earth
A voice that transcends the boundaries of language and birth
A voice that sings of the mysteries of life and death
A voice that echoes the silence of the breath

It is the voice of the Tibetan throat singers
The masters of the harmonic overtones
The keepers of the ancient wisdom
The seekers of the unknown

They sing with two or more notes at once
Creating a symphony of sound and vibration
They sing with the power of their lungs
Creating a harmony of body and mind

They sing to the mountains and the skies
To the spirits and the ancestors
To the sun and the moon
To the stars and the cosmos

They sing to express their joy and sorrow
Their faith and doubt
Their love and pain
Their hope and fear

They sing to connect with the source of all
The essence of being
The energy of life
The void of nothing

They sing to me and I listen
I feel their voice in my soul
I sense their presence in my heart
I share their vision in my mind

They sing to me and I wonder
What is the meaning of their song?
What is the purpose of their quest?
What is the secret of their art?

They sing to me and I answer
With my own voice and my own words
With my own thoughts and my own feelings
With my own questions and my own search

We sing together and we create
A dialogue of sound and silence
A bridge of culture and time
A bond of spirit and flesh

Shibuya: Where the Cosmic Flow Meets the City

At Shibuya Crossing in Tokyo, I stand and wait
For the signal to change and let me cross
The busy street, where thousands congregate
To move and mingle, unaware of loss

I wonder what they seek, these restless souls
Who hurry to their destinations, blind
To the beauty and the mystery that unfolds
Around them, in the city and the mind

Do they ever pause and question why
They live and breathe and love and die?
Do they ever sense the cosmic flow
That binds us all, above and below?

The light turns green, and I join the crowd
That surges forward, like a tidal wave
I feel the pulse of life, so strong and loud
That drowns out every doubt and fear I have

I see the faces, young and old and bright
That flash before me, like a kaleidoscope
Each one a story, a spark of light
That fills me with a sudden surge of hope

They may not know the answers, nor do I
But still they try to live and love and die
They may not see the cosmic flow
But still they feel it, in their soul

I reach the other side, and turn around
To see the spectacle once more
The crossing is a stage, where life is found
In all its colors, shapes and forms

I marvel at the diversity and grace
That fills the space, like a symphony
Each one a note, a part of a larger piece
That plays the music of humanity

They may not speak the same language, nor do I
But still they share the sound of life and joy
They may not hear the cosmic flow
But still they make it, with their voice

I walk away, and explore the city
That never sleeps, that never stops
The streets are filled with wonders and beauty
That catch my eye, and make me stop

I see the buildings, tall and sleek and proud
That touch the sky, like fingers of a hand
Each one a symbol, a statement loud
That speaks of progress and of grand

They may not last forever, nor will I
But still they stand and reach and try
They may not touch the cosmic flow
But still they shape it, with their hand

I see the shops, the cafes and the bars
That offer goods, and drinks and food
Each one a world, a planet full of stars
That shine and lure, and set the mood

I see the people, who enter and exit

Who buy and sell, and drink and eat
Each one a consumer, a seeker of a bit
Of pleasure and of comfort and of heat

They may not find fulfillment, nor will I
But still they search and taste and buy
They may not feed the cosmic flow
But still they savor it, with their mouth

I see the parks, the gardens and the shrines
That offer peace, and green and calm
Each one a refuge, a haven in the times
Of stress and noise and harm

I see the people, who sit and walk and pray
Who rest and breathe, and meditate
Each one a pilgrim, a traveler on the way
Of healing and of grace and of faith

They may not reach nirvana, nor will I
But still they hope and heal and try
They may not join the cosmic flow
But still they sense it, with their heart

I see the art, the culture and the history
That offer meaning, and depth and awe
Each one a treasure, a legacy of a story
That tells of who we are and what we saw

I see the people, who admire and create
Who learn and teach, and express

Each one a artist, a maker of a state
Of beauty and of truth and of impress

They may not capture reality, nor will I
But still they dream and craft and try
They may not show the cosmic flow
But still they reveal it, with their eye

I see the night, the darkness and the mystery
That offer wonder, and thrill and fear
Each one a challenge, a test of our ability
To face the unknown and the near

I see the people, who dare and risk and play
Who love and fight, and explore
Each one a hero, a warrior of a day
Who lives the moment and the more

They may not conquer the world, nor will I
But still they live and dare and try
They may not rule the cosmic flow
But still they ride it, with their will

I see myself, a stranger and a friend
A part of all, and yet alone
Each one a mirror, a reflection of an end
That waits for me and everyone

I do not know the purpose, nor do I
But still I live and love and die
I do not own the cosmic flow

But still I am it, with my soul

The Paradox of Being a Source and a Seeker

You are a giver of love, a healer of wounds
You share your light with those in the dark
You lend your ear to those who need to speak
You offer your hand to those who seek to rise
You are a source of strength, a fountain of hope

But do not forget that you are also human
You have your own needs, your own desires
You have your own dreams, your own fears
You have your own limits, your own flaws
You are not a machine, you are not a saint

You need to care for yourself, as much as you care for others
You need to help yourself, as much as you help others
You need to comfort yourself, as much as you comfort others
You need to support yourself, as much as you support others
You are important, you are valuable

You cannot pour from an empty cup, you cannot burn without fuel
You cannot heal without rest, you cannot grow without change
You cannot give without receiving, you cannot love without self-
love
You cannot be there for others, if you are not there for yourself
You are worthy, you are enough

You are not selfish, if you take some time for yourself
You are not weak, if you ask for some help
You are not rude, if you set some boundaries
You are not cold, if you say no sometimes
You are human, you are alive

You are not alone, you have people who care for you
You are not a burden, you have people who appreciate you
You are not a failure, you have people who admire you
You are not a mistake, you have people who love you
You are part of a community, you are part of a family

You have a purpose, you have a role
You have a voice, you have a choice
You have a vision, you have a mission
You have a passion, you have a reason

You have a life, you have a soul

You have a journey, you have a path
You have a past, you have a present
You have a future, you have a destiny
You have a challenge, you have a chance
You have a story, you have a legacy

You are a seeker of truth, a learner of wisdom
You explore the world with curiosity and wonder
You question the norms with courage and logic
You discover yourself with honesty and introspection
You are a thinker, you are a creator

Care for others, but don't leave yourself behind
Help them, but keep your own wellbeing in mind
Create comfort for them, but don't lose yourself on the way
Be their support, but don't forget yourself
You're important. To nurture others better, start with nurturing
yourself first.

The Unproven Self: A Poem of Existential Affirmation

What is the point of proving yourself
To the eyes that judge and the mouths that scorn?
What is the value of their approval
When they do not know the path you have borne?

You are the only one who can measure
The worth of your deeds and the depth of your soul
You are the only one who can treasure
The beauty of your dreams and the strength of your role

You do not have to prove anything to anyone
But yourself.

Why do you seek validation from others
When they have their own agendas and biases?
Why do you let them define your worth
When they have no clue of your struggles and sacrifices?

You are the only one who can affirm
The truth of your beliefs and the scope of your vision
You are the only one who can confirm
The joy of your achievements and the impact of your mission

You do not have to prove anything to anyone
But yourself.

How can you expect others to understand
The complexity of your thoughts and the subtlety of your feelings?
How can you hope others to appreciate
The uniqueness of your personality and the diversity of your
dealings?

You are the only one who can comprehend
The logic of your mind and the passion of your heart
You are the only one who can transcend

The limits of your body and the boundaries of your art

You do not have to prove anything to anyone
But yourself.

What is the use of conforming to norms
When they stifle your creativity and suppress your voice?
What is the gain of following the crowd
When they dull your senses and restrict your choice?

You are the only one who can create
The rules of your game and the style of your expression
You are the only one who can innovate
The methods of your work and the forms of your impression

You do not have to prove anything to anyone
But yourself.

Why do you fear the criticism of others
When they have their own flaws and insecurities?
Why do you let them influence your mood
When they have no power over your happiness and serenity?

You are the only one who can cope
With the challenges of life and the trials of fate
You are the only one who can hope
For the best of outcomes and the highest of state

You do not have to prove anything to anyone
But yourself.

How can you trust the opinions of others
When they have their own perspectives and prejudices?
How can you rely on their feedback
When they have no insight into your motives and objectives?

You are the only one who can judge
The quality of your actions and the morality of your conduct
You are the only one who can budge
The course of your destiny and the direction of your impact

You do not have to prove anything to anyone
But yourself.

What is the purpose of competing with others
When they have their own goals and priorities?
What is the benefit of comparing yourself
When they have no relevance to your abilities and realities?

You are the only one who can compete
With your own standards and your own potential
You are the only one who can compare
Your past performance and your future eventual

You do not have to prove anything to anyone
But yourself.

Why do you care about the expectations of others
When they have their own agendas and interests?
Why do you let them dictate your decisions

When they have no authority over your rights and requests?

You are the only one who can decide
The meaning of your life and the value of your purpose
You are the only one who can abide
By the principles of your faith and the ethics of your service

You do not have to prove anything to anyone
But yourself.

You are the master of your own destiny
The captain of your own ship
The author of your own story
The artist of your own masterpiece

You are the only one who can live
The life that you have chosen and the life that you deserve
You are the only one who can give
The gift that you have been given and the gift that you preserve

You do not have to prove anything to anyone
But yourself.

The Gift of Love: How You Made Me Feel Alive and Free

You opened my eyes to beauty sublime
When you came into my life like a ray of light
You showed me the wonders of this world and time
And filled my heart with joy and delight

You taught me to question and to seek the truth
To not be bound by dogma or creed
You inspired me to explore and to grow in youth
To not be afraid of doubt or need

You shared with me your dreams and your fears
Your hopes and your struggles, your joys and your tears
You made me feel that I was not alone
That we were connected by a bond unknown

You challenged me to think and to create
To express myself in words and art
You encouraged me to love and to relate
To open myself in mind and heart

You gave me a reason to live and to be
To face the world with courage and grace
You showed me a vision of what I could see
If I looked beyond the surface and the face

You helped me to discover who I am
To find my purpose and my place
You accepted me for what I am
And loved me with your kindness and your grace

You made me realize that life is a gift
That every moment is precious and rare
You showed me how to cherish and to uplift
The ones who matter and who care

You are the source of my happiness and peace
The one who makes me feel alive and free
You are the essence of my love and bliss
The one who completes and fulfills me

You are the beauty that I never knew
The love that I never felt
You are the miracle that came true
The one who made my heart melt

The Secret Harmony of Love

You are the hidden song that plays
When all the other tracks are done
The one that only those who stay
Can hear and appreciate its grace
You are the melody that stays
In my mind when the music's gone

The one that fills the empty space
With beauty and meaning in its trace
You are the secret song that sways
My soul with every note and tone

You are the bonus track that shines
When the album seems to be complete
The one that adds a new dimension
To the whole artistic expression
You are the harmony that binds
The disparate sounds into a suite
The one that elevates the tension
To a higher level of intention
You are the bonus track that finds
A way to make the album sweet

You are the hidden gem that glows
When the album cover is closed
The one that only those who seek
Can discover and admire its peak
You are the sparkle that bestows
A touch of magic to the prose
The one that makes the words unique
And gives them power when they speak
You are the hidden gem that shows
The depth of what the album knows

You are the bonus verse that flows
When the poem seems to end
The one that adds a twist or surprise
To the final message or advice
You are the rhythm that grows
The impact of the poem's trend
The one that amplifies the voice
And makes the reader rejoice

You are the bonus verse that knows
How to make the poem transcend

You are the hidden scene that plays
When the movie credits roll
The one that only those who wait
Can watch and appreciate its role
You are the story that stays
In my heart when the movie's over
The one that fills the missing hole
With emotion and meaning in its core
You are the hidden scene that sways
My mind with every scene and cover

You are the bonus chapter that shines
When the book seems to be done
The one that adds a new perspective
To the whole narrative objective
You are the plot that binds
The disparate events into one
The one that elevates the conflict
To a higher level of verdict
You are the bonus chapter that finds
A way to make the book fun

You are the hidden painting that glows
When the gallery lights are dimmed
The one that only those who look
Can see and admire its hook
You are the color that bestows
A touch of beauty to the grim
The one that makes the painting unique
And gives it power when it speaks
You are the hidden painting that shows
The depth of what the gallery thinks

You are the bonus puzzle that flows
When the game seems to be solved
The one that adds a new challenge
To the final outcome or balance
You are the logic that grows
The difficulty of the game's curve
The one that amplifies the chance
And makes the player advance
You are the bonus puzzle that knows
How to make the game evolve

You are the hidden song that plays
The bonus track that shines
The hidden gem that glows
The bonus verse that flows
The hidden scene that plays
The bonus chapter that shines
The hidden painting that glows
The bonus puzzle that flows
You are the hidden bonus that stays
In my life and makes it divine

The Human Condition: A Poem of Struggle and Meaning

When you are surrounded by chaos and strife
When the world seems to be out of control
Do not lose your nerve or your vision
But hold on to the truth that transcends all

That nothing lasts forever, not even pain
That every storm will eventually clear
That order will emerge from the chaos again
That hope will overcome the darkest fear

That this is the cycle of life and death
That we are but specks in the cosmic flow
That we must cherish every fleeting breath
But also learn to let go

When everything is falling apart
When you feel helpless and alone
Do not despair or lose your heart
But trust in the strength that is your own

That you have the power to endure and survive
That you have the wisdom to adapt and grow
That you have the courage to face and thrive
That you have the grace to accept and know

That this is the challenge of being human
That we are shaped by our trials and tests
That we must strive to find our meaning
But also embrace our limits

When the world is in chaos and disorder
When you see violence and injustice everywhere
Do not succumb to anger or fear
But stand for what is right and fair

That you have the voice to speak and protest
That you have the vision to imagine and create
That you have the will to act and resist
That you have the compassion to heal and relate

That this is the responsibility of being free
That we are accountable for our choices and deeds
That we must fight for our dignity
But also respect our differences

The Wind of Art : The River of Self

Rejoice in life, but do not lose your sight
Of what is real, and what is mere illusion
For joy is fleeting, like a flash of light
That fades away in darkness and confusion

Seek not the bliss that comes from false belief

But rather find the truth that sets you free
For faith is fragile, like a withered leaf
That falls and crumbles in the winter breeze

Embrace the world, but do not be enslaved
By its allure, and its deceptive charms
For wealth is transient, like a wave
That breaks and vanishes in the ocean's arms

Cherish your love, but do not be consumed
By its desire, and its consuming fire
For love is fickle, like a flower bloomed
That wilts and dies in time's relentless ire

Explore yourself, but do not be obsessed
By your own ego, and your own reflection
For self is fluid, like a river crested
That flows and changes in each new direction

Create your art, but do not be confined
By its form, and its rigid rules
For art is dynamic, like a wind
That shapes and shifts in endless moods

Learn from the past, but do not be trapped
By its memory, and its haunting scars
For past is gone, like a dream that snapped
That leaves behind only faint and fading stars

Dream of the future, but do not be fooled
By its promise, and its false hope
For future is unknown, like a path that cools
That leads to nowhere or a slippery slope

Live in the present, but do not be blind

By its reality, and its harsh demands
For present is precious, like a jewel that shines
That holds the key to both your heart and hands

Pickles: The Sour Spoilers of Life

You know what sucks? Pickles
You and I can't relate if you find pleasure in that abominable taste
They are the product of decay, of rotting and fermentation
A symbol of corruption, of moral degradation
They infect every dish, every meal, every occasion
They make me sick and angry, they stir up my frustration

They are the embodiment of all that I despise
They are the bitter tears in life's otherwise bright eyes
They are the pickles of existence, the curse of my role

You know what sucks? Pickles
You and I can't connect if you savor that repulsive green
They are the result of waste, of discarding and rejection
A sign of imperfection, of flawed selection
They spoil every bite, every flavor, every sensation
They make me sad and hopeless, they drain my motivation
They are the manifestation of all that I regret
They are the broken dreams in life's otherwise hopeful net
They are the pickles of existence, the toll of my goal

You know what sucks? Pickles
You and I can't converse if you praise that detestable crunch
They are the consequence of haste, of rushing and impatience
A mark of negligence, of poor maintenance
They mar every texture, every quality, every nuance
They make me dull and bored, they dull my intelligence
They are the illustration of all that I ignore
They are the missed opportunities in life's otherwise open door
They are the pickles of existence, the hole in my whole

You know what sucks? Pickles
You and I can't communicate if you admire that loathsome smell
They are the effect of change, of altering and transformation
A token of estrangement, of alienation
They clash with every aroma, every scent, every fragrance
They make me numb and distant, they sever my attachment
They are the representation of all that I avoid
They are the hidden fears in life's otherwise confident stride
They are the pickles of existence, the mole in my role

You know what sucks? Pickles

You and I can't bond if you cherish that odious sight
They are the outcome of chance, of random and variation
A trace of difference, of deviation
They contrast with every color, every hue, every shade
They make me blind and indifferent, they dim my vision
They are the expression of all that I deny
They are the ugly truths in life's otherwise beautiful lie
They are the pickles of existence, the coal in my bowl

You know what sucks? Pickles
You and I can't love if you adore that atrocious thing
They are the end of grace, of beauty and harmony
A loss of elegance, of symmetry
They disturb every balance, every proportion, every measure
They make me cold and hateful, they kill my pleasure
They are the confession of all that I hate
They are the unrequited feelings in life's otherwise passionate fate
They are the pickles of existence, the dole of my soul

You know what sucks? Pickles
You and I can't live if you worship that monstrous creation
They are the death of life, of growth and vitality
A lack of energy, of vitality
They hinder every movement, every action, every gesture
They make me weak and weary, they hinder my adventure
They are the admission of all that I fear
They are the inevitable endings in life's otherwise endless sphere
They are the pickles of existence, the pole of my role

You know what sucks? Pickles
You and I can't be if you accept that horrible reality
They are the void of meaning, of purpose and value
A absence of significance, of virtue
They negate every reason, every logic, every argument
They make me lost and confused, they shatter my enlightenment

They are the revelation of all that I doubt
They are the existential questions in life's otherwise certain route
They are the pickles of existence, the null of my soul

The Rug of Lies and the Voice of Truth

Don't let them silence your voice with their lies
Don't let them trample your dignity with their cries
Don't let them make you feel guilty for your choice
Don't let them take away your freedom with their ploys

You have the right to speak your mind and be heard

You have the right to assert your will and be served
You have the right to question their actions and motives
You have the right to demand their respect and notices

Sweeping under the rug is not a solution
It only breeds more resentment and confusion
Things don't improve by magic or by chance
They only change by effort and by stance

If you matter to them, they will understand
They will listen to your concerns and lend a hand
They will apologize for their mistakes and make amends
They will value your opinions and be your friends

But if you don't matter to them, they will ignore
They will dismiss your feelings and ask for more
They will justify their faults and blame you instead
They will disregard your views and be your dread

You will learn where you stand with them by their response
You will see their true colors by their conduct
You will know their real intentions by their words
You will judge their character by their deeds

Don't be afraid to stand for yourself and hold them accountable
Don't be afraid to confront them and make them responsible
Don't be afraid to challenge them and expose them
Don't be afraid to leave them and lose them

You are not alone in this world of strife
You are not alone in this journey of life
You are not alone in this quest of meaning
You are not alone in this dream of being

You have yourself and your inner strength

You have yourself and your moral sense
You have yourself and your creative spark
You have yourself and your guiding mark

You are the master of your own destiny
You are the maker of your own reality
You are the seeker of your own truth
You are the lover of your own self

You Are My Music, You Are My Art

You are the melody that lingers in my mind
The harmony that fills my soul with bliss
You are the rhythm that pulses through my veins
The tune that makes me feel alive and free

You are the words that speak to my heart

The verses that inspire me to grow
You are the rhyme that gives my life meaning
The chorus that echoes in my dreams

You are the song that transcends time and space
The symphony that connects us beyond death
You are the music that I seek and cherish
The lyrics that I write and sing for you

You are the light that guides me in the dark
The flame that warms me in the cold
You are the spark that ignites my passion
The fire that burns in my eyes and soul

You are the color that paints my world
The hue that brightens my mood
You are the shade that contrasts my thoughts
The tint that enriches my view

You are the art that beautifies my life
The masterpiece that captivates me
You are the brush that strokes my canvas
The paint that blends with my spirit

You are the flower that blooms in my garden
The fragrance that delights my senses
You are the seed that sprouts in my soil
The fruit that nourishes my body and mind

You are the nature that surrounds me
The force that sustains me
You are the wind that caresses my skin
The rain that cleanses my soul

You are the earth that grounds me

The sky that lifts me
You are the sun that shines on me
The moon that watches over me

You are the star that twinkles in my night
The comet that dazzles me with your flight
You are the galaxy that expands my horizons
The universe that holds me in your embrace

The Art of Happiness: A Poetic Guide to Productivity

Happiness is the key to unlock the door
Of productivity and creativity galore
But happiness is not a thing to be found
It is a state of mind, a way to be bound

To the present moment, the here and the now
Not to the past regrets or the future vows
But to the beauty and wonder of life as it is
To the joys and sorrows that make us human
To the love and compassion that connect us all

Happiness is not a reward for our deeds
Nor a punishment for our misdeeds
It is a choice that we make every day
To see the positive or the negative in our way
To be grateful or resentful for what we have
To be hopeful or fearful for what we crave
To be content or restless with who we are
To be authentic or pretentious with our star
To be happy or unhappy with our fate

Happiness is not a destination to reach
Nor a lesson to learn or a sermon to preach
It is a journey that we take every step
To explore the unknown or the known with pep
To embrace the challenges or the opportunities
To overcome the obstacles or the adversities
To grow and learn from our mistakes
To share and give from our heartaches
To live and love from our soul

Happiness is not a commodity to buy
Nor a luxury to enjoy or a right to deny
It is a necessity that we need every breath
To survive the hardships or the ease with zest
To nourish our body or our mind
To heal our wounds or our scars
To energize our spirit or our will
To inspire our dreams or our goals
To create our reality or our bliss

Happiness is not a competition to win
Nor a comparison to make or a sin to commit
It is a collaboration that we seek every touch
To support each other or ourselves with much
To respect our differences or our similarities
To appreciate our diversity or our unity
To celebrate our successes or our failures
To acknowledge our strengths or our weaknesses
To accept our flaws or our perfections

Happiness is not a static state to maintain
Nor a dynamic state to change or a pain to sustain
It is a fluid state that we flow every move
To adapt to the situations or the conditions with groove
To be flexible or rigid with our plans
To be open or closed with our views
To be curious or bored with our quests
To be adventurous or cautious with our risks
To be spontaneous or predictable with our actions

Happiness is not a feeling to chase
Nor a thought to control or a mood to erase
It is a sensation that we sense every moment
To be aware of our emotions or our thoughts with intent
To be mindful or distracted with our focus
To be attentive or negligent with our awareness
To be conscious or unconscious with our choices
To be deliberate or impulsive with our voices
To be expressive or repressive with our feelings

Happiness is not a privilege to claim
Nor a duty to perform or a blame to assign
It is a responsibility that we bear every word
To be accountable for our actions or our reactions with accord

To be honest or dishonest with our intentions
To be ethical or unethical with our decisions
To be moral or immoral with our values
To be fair or unfair with our judgments
To be kind or unkind with our words

Happiness is not a secret to discover
Nor a mystery to solve or a puzzle to uncover
It is a reality that we create every thought
To be positive or negative with our attitude with ought
To be optimistic or pessimistic with our outlook
To be constructive or destructive with our input
To be proactive or reactive with our approach
To be solution-oriented or problem-oriented with our coach
To be happy or unhappy with our thought

The Circle that Limits Your Greatness

A circle is a shape of harmony and grace
A symbol of perfection and completeness
But what if it becomes a trap, a prison for your soul
A limit to your vision and your goals?

What if your circle does not challenge you to grow

To seek new heights and depths, to learn and know
What if your circle only feeds your fears and doubts
And keeps you in the comfort of the known?

What if your circle does not inspire you to create
To express your inner self, to innovate
What if your circle only stifles your imagination
And makes you conform to its expectations?

What if your circle does not support you to achieve
To pursue your dreams and passions, to believe
What if your circle only holds you back from success
And makes you settle for mediocrity?

What if your circle does not respect you as you are
To value your uniqueness, to admire
What if your circle only judges you by its standards
And makes you feel inadequate and inferior?

What if your circle does not love you unconditionally
To accept your flaws and mistakes, to forgive
What if your circle only hurts you with its words and deeds
And makes you feel unworthy and unloved?

What if your circle does not enrich you with its diversity
To expose you to new perspectives, to enlighten
What if your circle only isolates you from the world
And makes you ignorant and narrow-minded?

What if your circle does not empower you to change
To transform yourself and others, to make a difference
What if your circle only resists your evolution
And makes you stagnant and complacent?

What if your circle does not push you to become great

To realize your potential, to transcend
What if your circle only confines you to its boundaries
And makes you a prisoner of its cage?

The Paradox of Philosophy

Philosophy is the quest for wisdom
But wisdom is not the same as virtue
For virtue is a matter of opinion
And opinion is a shifting view

Philosophy is the love of knowledge

But knowledge is not the same as truth
For truth is a matter of evidence
And evidence is a fleeting proof

Philosophy is the art of thinking
But thinking is not the same as being
For being is a matter of existence
And existence is a fleeting thing

Philosophy is the science of reason
But reason is not the same as logic
For logic is a matter of deduction
And deduction is a narrow trick

Philosophy is the craft of language
But language is not the same as meaning
For meaning is a matter of interpretation
And interpretation is a biased leaning

Philosophy is the skill of argument
But argument is not the same as dialogue
For dialogue is a matter of communication
And communication is a complex slog

Philosophy is the discipline of inquiry
But inquiry is not the same as curiosity
For curiosity is a matter of interest
And interest is a subjective quality

Philosophy is the practice of reflection
But reflection is not the same as introspection
For introspection is a matter of self-awareness
And self-awareness is a rare perfection

Philosophy is the pursuit of enlightenment

But enlightenment is not the same as salvation
For salvation is a matter of faith
And faith is a personal conviction

The Lion's Paradox: A Poem of Humility and Strength

Be fierce and brave, but not too proud
For pride can blind you from the truth
That life is fleeting, like a cloud
That changes shape with every breath

Some people will not care for you
They will exploit your trust and kindness
They will not see your point of view
They will not value your uniqueness

Always know when to stand your ground
When to resist and when to yield
When to speak up and when to sound
The silent wisdom of the field

But do not let your anger grow
Into a flame that burns your soul
For anger only feeds the woe
That makes you feel less than whole

Seek instead the inner peace
That comes from knowing who you are
That you are more than what you see
That you are part of something larger

But do not lose yourself in awe
Of mysteries that lie beyond
For mystery is not a law
That you must blindly follow on

Question everything you know
But do not doubt your own existence
For you are here to learn and grow
To find your purpose and your essence

But do not think you know it all
For knowledge is a endless quest
That leads you to new paths and walls
That challenge you to do your best

Be humble and admit your flaws
But do not let them define you
For you are more than what you cause
You are what you aspire to

Be like a lion, but be humble
For humility is not a weakness
It is a strength that makes you humble
It is a virtue that makes you fearless

The Art of Concealment : Masks and Truths

What do you gain by revealing your soul
To those who do not care or understand?
They will only judge, mock, or take control
Of the secrets that you hold in your hand.

Better to keep them hidden in the dark

Where they are safe from prying eyes and ears
And only let them out when you embark
On a journey with someone who endears.

But even then, be careful what you share
For trust is fragile and can break at will
And once it's gone, you cannot repair
The damage that was done by being still.

You may think that honesty is the best
But sometimes it can put you to the test.

Do not mistake your silence for a flaw
It is a strength that many do not have
You do not need to fill the air with words
That only serve to make the others laugh.

You have a depth that they cannot fathom
A richness that they cannot comprehend
You do not need to lower your standards
To fit in with the shallow and the bland.

You have a voice that speaks when it matters
A wisdom that comes from within
You do not need to follow the chatter
That only leads to folly and to sin.

You may think that speaking is a skill
But sometimes it can make you look like nil.

Why do you seek approval from the crowd

When they do not know who you really are?
They will only praise you when you're loud
And then forget you when you're not a star.

You have a value that is not defined
By the opinions of the masses
You have a purpose that is not confined
By the expectations of the classes.

You have a vision that is not blurred
By the illusions of the world
You have a mission that is not deterred
By the obstacles that are hurled.

You may think that popularity is a goal
But sometimes it can take away your soul.

How do you cope with the loneliness
That comes from being different and unique?
You do not find solace in the commonness
That others seek to make them feel less weak.

You have a friend that is always with you
A companion that never leaves your side
You have yourself, the one who knows you true
A confidant that never has to hide.

You have a joy that is not dependent
On the presence of another
You have a peace that is not contingent
On the approval of a brother.

You may think that solitude is a curse

But sometimes it can be a source of verse.

What do you fear by facing your own self
The one who knows your flaws and your mistakes?
You do not need to put him on a shelf
And pretend that he does not exist.

You have a chance to learn from your errors
A opportunity to grow and improve
You have a choice to overcome your terrors
A responsibility to make a move.

You have a power that is not limited
By the constraints of your past
You have a potential that is not inhibited
By the doubts that you cast.

You may think that self-awareness is a pain
But sometimes it can be a way to gain.

Where do you find meaning in your life
When everything seems pointless and absurd?
You do not need to look for it in strife
Or in the promises of a false word.

You have a passion that is not quenched
By the futility of existence
You have a creativity that is not clenched
By the absurdity of resistance.

You have a beauty that is not marred

By the ugliness of reality
You have a grace that is not scarred
By the cruelty of humanity.

You may think that meaning is a myth
But sometimes it can be a source of bliss.

When do you feel alive in your being
When everything seems dull and mundane?
You do not need to wait for a feeling
Or for a moment that is inane.

You have a spark that is not dimmed
By the monotony of routine
You have a fire that is not skimmed
By the mediocrity of the scene.

You have a zest that is not dampened
By the boredom of the day
You have a spirit that is not hampered
By the inertia of the way.

You may think that living is a chore
But sometimes it can be a way to soar.

Who do you love in your heart of hearts
When everyone seems distant and cold?
You do not need to search for it in parts
Or in the fragments that you hold.

You have a love that is not divided

By the walls that you erect
You have a love that is not misguided
By the fears that you project.

You have a love that is not conditional
On the reciprocation of another
You have a love that is not irrational
On the validation of a lover.

You may think that love is a rare find
But sometimes it can be a state of mind.

How do you live in this world of masks
Where everyone hides behind a face?
You do not need to join them in their tasks
Or in their games of deceit and disgrace.

You have a truth that is not concealed
By the lies that you tell
You have a truth that is not revealed
By the masks that you sell.

You have a truth that is not compromised
By the pressures of society
You have a truth that is not disguised
By the pretenses of propriety.

You may think that truth is a dangerous thing
But sometimes it can be a way to sing.

The Hopelessness of Loving the Hateful

The ones who seek their own demise
Are often blind to friendly eyes
They spurn the hands that reach to save
And curse the ones who dare to brave
The stormy seas of their despair
The dark abyss of their nightmare

They do not want to see the light
They only crave the endless night
They hate you for your hope and care

You wonder why they are so cold
You wonder what has made them bold
To face the pain of self-inflicted wounds
To shun the love that tries to soothe
The broken pieces of their soul
The shattered fragments of their whole
You wonder what has made them choose
To lose the life they could renew
You wonder what has made them lose

You try to understand their plight
You try to empathize with their fight
But you cannot grasp the reason why
They want to live as if to die
You cannot fathom their despair
You cannot measure their nightmare
You only see the wasted life
You only see the needless strife
You only see the hopeless stare

You wish you could make them see
You wish you could make them free
From the chains that bind them to their fate
From the lies that make them hate
The ones who offer them a chance
The ones who ask them for a dance
You wish you could make them smile
You wish you could make them stay awhile
You wish you could make them glance

But they are not like you and me

They are not like us who see
The beauty of the world around
The joy of the life we've found
They are not like us who feel
The warmth of the love that's real
They are not like us who know
The grace of the time that flows
They are not like us who heal

They are like the fallen leaves
They are like the barren trees
They have no color in their sight
They have no greenery in their plight
They have no fragrance in their smell
They have no springtime in their hell
They have no music in their ears
They have no melody in their fears
They have no rhythm in their spell

They are like the dying stars
They are like the fading scars
They have no light in their heart
They have no fire in their art
They have no warmth in their touch
They have no passion in their clutch
They have no spark in their mind
They have no brilliance in their kind
They have no glow in their much

They are like the broken glass
They are like the rusted brass
They have no shape in their form
They have no strength in their storm
They have no shine in their face
They have no elegance in their grace

They have no smoothness in their edge
They have no sharpness in their wedge
They have no polish in their trace

They are like the empty space
They are like the silent place
They have no matter in their being
They have no sound in their meaning
They have no substance in their core
They have no voice in their roar
They have no depth in their dimension
They have no echo in their tension
They have no presence in their more

Riddles and Scripts

    You cannot solve the riddles
Of someone else's life
You cannot rewrite the scripts
That make them laugh or cry

You cannot alter the events

That shaped their history
You cannot undo the effects
That left them in misery

You cannot cure their ailments
Or ease their agony
You cannot restore their health
By giving them your sympathy

But you can offer them a place
Where they can rest and breathe
You can share with them your grace
And show them hospitality

You can hear their stories
And acknowledge their feelings
You can honor their memories
And support their healing

You can stand beside them
And journey with them along the way
You can lend them your wisdom
And help them find their way

But they have to make the choices
To improve their situation
They have to face the noises
And overcome their frustration

They have to find their courage
And reclaim their dignity
They have to seek their meaning
And discover their destiny

They have to heal themselves

And create their own happiness
They have to love themselves
And embrace their own uniqueness

You cannot fix their problems for them
No matter how much you adore
You cannot change their past for them
Or make their troubles vanish

But you can be their companion and friend
And share their dreams and hopes
You can be their light and guide
And inspire them to cope

The Question of God: A Poem Inspired by Stephen Hawking

I.

What is the origin of the cosmos?
What is the meaning of existence?

What is the fate of the universe?
These are the questions that haunt us
The questions that science tries to answer
But can science explain everything?
Is there a place for God in the equation?
Or is God just a human invention?
A way to cope with the unknown?

II.

Stephen Hawking was a brilliant mind
A physicist who explored the mysteries of time and space
He sought to understand the laws of nature
And the secrets of the big bang and black holes
He did not believe in a personal God
A God who intervenes in human affairs
He did not need God to explain the world
He relied on reason and evidence

III.

He said that the universe is governed by natural laws
That can be discovered and tested by observation and experiment
He said that the universe is self-contained and self-sufficient
That it does not need a creator or a cause
He said that the universe is not designed or fine-tuned
That it is the result of random fluctuations and quantum mechanics
He said that the universe is not eternal or infinite
That it has a beginning and an end

IV.

He challenged the traditional views of religion
He questioned the existence and role of God
He argued that God is not necessary or compatible

With the scientific understanding of reality
He claimed that God is a delusion or an illusion
A product of wishful thinking or fear
He asserted that God is irrelevant or obsolete
A concept that has no place in the modern world

V.

But is he right? Is he wrong?
Is he certain? Is he doubtful?
Is he arrogant? Is he humble?
Is he wise? Is he foolish?
Is he enlightened? Is he blind?
Is he free? Is he trapped?
Is he human? Is he divine?
Is he alive? Is he dead?

VI.

How do we know what is true?
How do we know what is real?
How do we know what is good?
How do we know what is beautiful?
How do we know what is right?
How do we know what is wrong?
How do we know what is God?
How do we know what is not?

VII.

Is there a way to reconcile science and religion?
Is there a way to harmonize reason and faith?
Is there a way to integrate nature and spirit?
Is there a way to bridge the gap between the physical and the
metaphysical?

Is there a way to find a common ground between the empirical and
the transcendental?
Is there a way to discover a shared truth between the objective and
the subjective?
Is there a way to encounter a living God between the immanent and
the transcendent?

VIII.

Some say that science and religion are complementary
That they address different aspects of reality
That they answer different questions of humanity
That they offer different perspectives of divinity
Some say that science and religion are compatible
That they can coexist and cooperate
That they can enrich and inspire
That they can reveal and illuminate

IX.

Some say that science and religion are in conflict
That they are opposed and incompatible
That they contradict and exclude
That they compete and undermine
Some say that science and religion are irrelevant
That they are outdated and obsolete
That they are meaningless and useless
That they are harmful and dangerous

X.

What do you say? What do you think?
What do you believe? What do you doubt?
What do you hope? What do you fear?
What do you love? What do you hate?

What do you seek? What do you find?
What do you lose? What do you gain?
What do you give? What do you take?
What do you live? What do you die?

XI.

The question of God is not a simple one
It is not a matter of yes or no
It is not a matter of black or white
It is not a matter of fact or opinion
It is a complex and profound one
It is a matter of mystery and wonder
It is a matter of nuance and depth
It is a matter of experience and relationship

XII.

The question of God is not a new one
It is as old as humanity itself
It is a universal and timeless one
It is shared by every culture and generation
It is a personal and existential one
It is rooted in our nature and destiny
It is a vital and urgent one
It is relevant to our life and death

XIII.

The question of God is not an easy one
It is not a question that can be answered by logic or evidence alone
It is not a question that can be settled by authority or tradition alone
It is not a question that can be solved by science or religion alone
It is a challenging and demanding one
It requires openness and humility

It requires curiosity and creativity
It requires dialogue and collaboration

XIV.

The question of God is not a final one
It is not a question that has a definitive or conclusive answer
It is not a question that has a fixed or static answer
It is not a question that has a single or universal answer
It is an ongoing and evolving one
It invites exploration and discovery
It invites reflection and revision
It invites diversity and plurality

XV.

The question of God is not a trivial one
It is not a question that can be ignored or dismissed
It is not a question that can be avoided or evaded
It is not a question that can be ridiculed or mocked
It is a serious and significant one
It has implications and consequences
It has meaning and purpose
It has value and dignity

XVI.

The question of God is not a lonely one
It is not a question that can be asked or answered in isolation
It is not a question that can be explored or expressed in solitude
It is not a question that can be experienced or enjoyed in seclusion
It is a communal and relational one
It connects us with others
It connects us with ourselves
It connects us with God

XVII.

The question of God is not a theoretical one
It is not a question that can be reduced to abstract concepts or ideas
It is not a question that can be confined to academic debates or discussions
It is not a question that can be detached from practical issues or concerns
It is a practical and ethical one
It affects how we live and act
It affects how we treat and respect
It affects how we love and serve

XVIII.

The question of God is not a passive one
It is not a question that can be answered by mere words or thoughts
It is not a question that can be explored by mere observation or analysis
It is not a question that can be experienced by mere feelings or emotions
It is an active and dynamic one
It demands action and response
It demands commitment and involvement
It demands transformation and growth

XIX.

The question of God is not a closed one
It is not a question that can be answered once and for all
It is not a question that can be explored to the fullest extent
It is not a question that can be experienced to the highest degree
It is an open and infinite one
It always leaves room for more

It always leaves room for surprise
It always leaves room for grace

The Calendar of Life

I.

No more a list of tasks to do
That mocks me with its endless length
And fills my mind with restless dread
Of wasted hours and waning strength

I choose a different way instead
To plan my days and nights anew
With blocks of time on my calendar
That give each task its rightful due
And help me reach my goals afar

II.

A block of time is not a cage
That traps me in a rigid frame
But rather a creative space
That lets me play a mindful game
Of balancing the work and grace
Of every moment and every stage
With blocks of time on my calendar
I can adjust and rearrange
And find the flow that suits my nature

III.

A block of time is not a race
That urges me to hurry on
But rather a reflective pause
That lets me breathe and linger on
The beauty and the meaning of
Each action and each interface
With blocks of time on my calendar
I can attend and appreciate
And savor the gifts that life offers

IV.

A block of time is not a chase
That drives me to compete and win
But rather a collaborative chance

That lets me learn and grow and sin
With others who can enhance
My vision and my skill and grace
With blocks of time on my calendar
I can connect and communicate
And build the bonds that matter

V.

A block of time is not a waste
That drains me of my energy
But rather a replenishing source
That lets me tap my synergy
With forces that can reinforce
My passion and my will and taste
With blocks of time on my calendar
I can align and integrate
And unleash the power that I harbor

VI.

A block of time is not a haste
That makes me miss the finer points
But rather a meticulous care
That lets me polish and anoint
The details that can make or break
My work and art and style and grace
With blocks of time on my calendar
I can refine and elevate
And master the craft that I prefer

VII.

A block of time is not a case
That judges me by what I do

But rather a liberating choice
That lets me be and feel and view
The world and myself with a voice
That speaks my truth and worth and grace
With blocks of time on my calendar
I can express and create
And share the gifts that I bear

VIII.

A block of time is not a maze
That confuses me with twists and turns
But rather a guiding light
That lets me see and know and learn
The path that leads me to the right
Direction and goal and pace
With blocks of time on my calendar
I can explore and navigate
And find the way that I desire

IX.

A block of time is not a phase
That fades away with changing trends
But rather a lasting legacy
That lets me leave a mark and end
The journey with a memory
That lives beyond my days and grace
With blocks of time on my calendar
I can contribute and celebrate
And make a difference that matters

X.

A block of time is not a blaze

That burns me out with stress and strain
But rather a soothing balm
That lets me heal and rest and gain
The peace and calm that can sustain
My health and joy and grace
With blocks of time on my calendar
I can relax and recuperate
And renew the strength that I cherish

XI.

A block of time is not a craze
That distracts me with noise and flash
But rather a mindful focus
That lets me filter and trash
The clutter and the fuss that can
Diminish my clarity and grace
With blocks of time on my calendar
I can prioritize and eliminate
And clear the space that I need

XII.

A block of time is not a glaze
That covers me with a dull veneer
But rather a vibrant hue
That lets me shine and glow and cheer
The colors and the shades that can
Enrich my life and grace
With blocks of time on my calendar
I can diversify and decorate
And brighten the place that I live

XIII.

A block of time is not a craze
That tempts me with a false allure
But rather a genuine value
That lets me seek and find and secure
The things and the people that can
Fulfill my needs and grace
With blocks of time on my calendar
I can select and accumulate
And treasure the wealth that I have

XIV.

A block of time is not a phase
That limits me with a fixed role
But rather a dynamic role
That lets me change and grow and evolve
The aspects and the facets that can
Define my identity and grace
With blocks of time on my calendar
I can transform and innovate
And shape the self that I am

XV.

A block of time is not a haze
That blinds me with a narrow view
But rather a wide perspective
That lets me see and know and review
The world and myself with a new
Insight and wisdom and grace
With blocks of time on my calendar
I can expand and update
And broaden the mind that I use

XVI.

A block of time is not a craze
That numbs me with a shallow thrill
But rather a deep satisfaction
That lets me feel and enjoy and fill
My heart and soul with a real
Emotion and meaning and grace
With blocks of time on my calendar
I can enrich and appreciate
And nourish the spirit that I have

XVII.

A block of time is not a phase
That isolates me with a wall
But rather a bridge that connects
That lets me reach and touch and call
The others who can affect
My life and happiness and grace
With blocks of time on my calendar
I can relate and communicate
And foster the relationships that I value

XVIII.

A block of time is not a craze
That consumes me with a single aim
But rather a balance that harmonizes
That lets me blend and mix and tame
The various elements that can
Enhance my quality and grace
With blocks of time on my calendar
I can integrate and moderate
And achieve the harmony that I seek

XIX.

A block of time is not a phrase
That sums up my life with a word
But rather a story that unfolds
That lets me live and tell and record
The events and the moments that can
Compose my legacy and grace
With blocks of time on my calendar
I can write and narrate
And create the life that I want

Remember, Think, Know: A Poem of Resilience

When the world seems to crumble around you
And you struggle to keep your head above water
When you feel the weight of your burdens crushing you
And you wonder if you can endure any longer

Remember this: you have faced worse before
Remember this: you have overcome many trials
Remember this: you have a resilience at your core
Remember this: you have a spark that never dies
Remember this: you are not alone in this fight

When the night is long and dark and cold
And you can't find a ray of hope or light
When you are haunted by the fears of old
And you can't sleep or rest or dream
Think of this: you have seen brighter days
Think of this: you have felt warmer suns
Think of this: you have known happier ways
Think of this: you have shared deeper bonds
Think of this: you will not be lost in the night

When the pain is sharp and deep and real
And you can't numb or heal or cope
When you are wounded by the words that people say
And you can't speak or smile or joke
Know this: you have endured harder blows
Know this: you have survived greater wounds
Know this: you have grown stronger through the woes
Know this: you have learned wiser from the fools
Know this: you will not be broken by the pain

When the doubt is loud and harsh and cruel
And you can't trust or believe or hope
When you are challenged by the tasks that life demands
And you can't work or play or cope
Tell yourself this: you have done more than you think
Tell yourself this: you have achieved more than you know
Tell yourself this: you have risen from the brink
Tell yourself this: you have shown more than you show
Tell yourself this: you will not be defeated by the doubt

When the change is fast and fierce and strange
And you can't adapt or grow or learn
When you are faced with the unknown and the new
And you can't explore or discover or discern
Remind yourself this: you have embraced more than you fear
Remind yourself this: you have transformed more than you stay
Remind yourself this: you have ventured beyond the near
Remind yourself this: you have found more than you seek
Remind yourself this: you will not be afraid of the change

When the loss is heavy and hard and sad
And you can't grieve or mourn or cry
When you are parted from the ones you love
And you can't hug or kiss or say goodbye
Hold on to this: you have loved more than you lose
Hold on to this: you have cherished more than you miss
Hold on to this: you have memories that won't fade
Hold on to this: you have a heart that won't break
Hold on to this: you will not be alone in the loss

When the joy is rare and brief and sweet
And you can't savor or enjoy or celebrate
When you are distracted by the troubles of the world
And you can't relax or unwind or appreciate
Look for this: you have reasons to be grateful
Look for this: you have moments to be happy
Look for this: you have blessings to be thankful
Look for this: you have friends to be merry
Look for this: you will not be deprived of the joy

When the future is uncertain and unclear and vague
And you can't plan or predict or prepare
When you are unsure of what lies ahead
And you can't envision or imagine or dare

Hope for this: you have potential to be great
Hope for this: you have opportunities to be brave
Hope for this: you have dreams to be fulfilled
Hope for this: you have a destiny to be shaped
Hope for this: you will not be disappointed by the future

When the present is hard and harsh and real
And you can't live or breathe or be
When you are overwhelmed by the now
And you can't face or accept or see
Live for this: you have a purpose to fulfill
Live for this: you have a passion to pursue
Live for this: you have a voice to express
Live for this: you have a choice to make
Live for this: you will not be wasted by the present

This one I'll never forget

Me crafting a new password

I stare at the blank screen, waiting for a sign
A word, a phrase, a code, that will be mine
Something that reflects my identity and soul
Something that no one else can ever know or control

But how can I capture the essence of my being
In a string of letters, numbers, and symbols, fleeting
How can I express the complexity of my mind
In a format that is simple, secure, and confined

I think of all the memories that shaped my life
The joys and sorrows, the peace and strife
The people I loved, the places I saw, the things I learned
The dreams I chased, the bridges I burned, the scars I earned

But none of them seem to fit the criteria
They are either too common, too vague, or too familiar
They do not convey the uniqueness of my existence
They do not reveal the depth of my persistence

I wonder if there is a point to this exercise
A purpose, a meaning, a value, behind this disguise
Is there a reason why I need to hide behind a mask
Is there a reward for completing this impossible task

But I cannot find an answer that satisfies me
I cannot escape the absurdity that I see
I cannot deny the futility of my action
I cannot defy the inevitability of my extinction

I realize that I am wasting my precious time
Time that could be spent on something sublime
Time that could be used to create and explore
Time that could be cherished before I am no more

But I have no choice but to follow the rules
The rules that are made by the powerful fools
The rules that are imposed on the weak and the meek
The rules that are absurd, unfair, and bleak

I decide to give up on my quest for perfection
I settle for a compromise, a random selection
I type in some characters, without rhyme or reason
I hope that they will last, until the next season

This one I'll never forget
Me crafting a new password
But I know that I will, like everything else
Like the dust in the wind, like the books on the shelves
Like the sun in the sky, like the stars in the night
Like the poem in my mind, like the password in my sight

The Art of Eating Less

I.

Why do you run so fast and far,
Chasing the elusive goal of health?
Why do you sweat and pant and jar
Your bones and muscles, wasting wealth

Of time and energy, when you can
Achieve the same result with ease
By simply following a plan
That does not make you wheeze and freeze?
The art of eating less is all you need.

II.

You think that by exerting more
You burn the calories you ate
But do you know the hidden score
That lies behind your changing fate?
The more you exercise, the more
You stimulate your appetite
And end up eating even more
Than what you did before the fight
The art of eating less is what you need.

III.

You may have heard of protein's power
To build your muscles and your strength
But do you know that every hour
You also need a certain length
Of time to digest and absorb
The amino acids in your food?
And if you eat too much, you rob
Your body of the chance to use
The art of eating less is how you need.

IV.

You may have learned of fiber's role
To keep your gut and colon clean
But do you know that fiber's goal

Is also to control your spleen?
By filling up your stomach's space
With bulky matter, fiber slows
Your hunger signals and your pace
Of eating, and thus it bestows
The art of eating less is when you need.

V.

You may admire the ancient Greeks
Who gave us art and science fair
But do you know that their physique
Was not the product of fresh air
And exercise alone, but more
The outcome of their frugal diet
They ate with moderation, bore
No gluttony, and thus they tried
The art of eating less is why you need.

VI.

You may revere the modern sages
Who dazzle us with wit and skill
But do you know that through the ages
They also practiced self-control
And discipline in what they ate
And drank, and thus they kept their mind
And body in a balanced state
And never let themselves be blind
The art of eating less is where you need.

VII.

You may aspire to be like them
The heroes of the past and present

But do you know that you can stem
The tide of fate with one consent
And one decision, to embrace
The simple rule of eating less
And thus to find the inner grace
And peace that comes with mindfulness
The art of eating less is who you need.

VIII.

You may wonder how to start
This journey of a thousand miles
But do you know that in your heart
You have the key to all the trials
And challenges that lie ahead
The key is to be aware
Of what you eat, and why, and shed
The habits that impair and scare
The art of eating less is what you need.

IX.

You may doubt if you can do
This feat of will and self-restraint
But do you know that it is true
That nothing is impossible
If you believe and persevere
And seek the help of those who care
And those who have the same idea
And vision, and who want to share
The art of eating less is how you need.

X.

You may think that eating less

Is boring and depriving
But do you know that eating less
Is also liberating and thriving
For when you eat less, you free
Yourself from the bondage of food
And when you eat less, you see
The beauty of the world and mood
The art of eating less is when you need.

XI.

You may fear that eating less
Will make you weak and frail
But do you know that eating less
Will make you strong and hale
For when you eat less, you give
Your body time to heal and rest
And when you eat less, you live
Longer and better, and you test
The art of eating less is why you need.

XII.

You may worry that eating less
Will make you miss the joys of life
But do you know that eating less
Will make you savor the spice of life
For when you eat less, you taste
The flavors and the textures more
And when you eat less, you waste
Less time and money, and you score
The art of eating less is where you need.

XIII.

You may wonder what to eat
When you decide to eat less
But do you know that you can eat
Whatever you like, as long as
You eat with moderation, and
You balance your nutrition, and
You listen to your body, and
You enjoy your food, and
The art of eating less is who you need.

XIV.

You may ask how much to eat
When you resolve to eat less
But do you know that you can eat
As much as you need, as long as
You eat slowly, and
You chew well, and
You stop when you are full, and
You do not overeat, and
The art of eating less is what you need.

XV.

You may wonder when to eat
When you commit to eat less
But do you know that you can eat
Whenever you want, as long as
You eat regularly, and
You do not skip meals, and
You do not snack too much, and
You do not eat too late, and
The art of eating less is how you need.

XVI.

You may wonder why to eat
When you choose to eat less
But do you know that you can eat
For many reasons, as long as
You eat for nourishment, and
You eat for pleasure, and
You eat for health, and
You do not eat for stress, and
The art of eating less is when you need.

XVII.

You may wonder where to eat
When you learn to eat less
But do you know that you can eat
Anywhere you like, as long as
You eat at the table, and
You do not eat in bed, and
You do not eat in front of the TV, and
You do not eat on the go, and
The art of eating less is where you need.

XVIII.

You may wonder who to eat
When you master eating less
But do you know that you can eat
With anyone you love, as long as
You eat with family, and
You eat with friends, and
You eat with yourself, and
You do not eat with enemies, and
The art of eating less is who you need.

XIX.

You may wonder what is the end
Of this long and winding road
But do you know that there is no end
Only a new beginning, a new mode
Of living and being, a new way
Of seeing and feeling, a new day
Of eating and loving, a new art
Of eating less, and a new heart
The art of eating less is all you need.

The Stolen Souls: A Song of the Jiang Shi's Curse

They lurk in the shadows of the night
With rigid limbs and papered skin
They hop and hop with no respite
In search of living blood to win

They are the stiff corpses of the lore
The jiang shi, the hopping dead
They heed the call of a dark power
That binds them to a sorcerer's will

They were once humans, long ago
But died in lands far from their home
Their souls could not depart in peace
And so they rose as undead beasts

They wear the clothes of ancient times
The robes and hats of dynasties past
They bear the seal of their master's crimes
The yellow talisman on their face

They have no mind, no will, no heart
They only know to obey and kill
They feel no pain, no fear, no smart
They only hop and hop until

They find a victim, unaware
They pounce and bite with fangs of steel
They drain the blood and life and air

They leave behind a lifeless shell

They are the scourge of the living world
The jiang shi, the hopping dread
They are the spawn of a twisted word
That animates the silent dead

They shun the light of the sun and moon
They hide in caves and tombs and wells
They only stir when darkness looms
They heed the sound of a ringing bell

They follow the lead of their master's hand
They hop and hop as he commands
They are his slaves, his tools, his band
They are his army, his force, his plan

He is the one who holds the key
The secret of the jiang shi's birth
He is the one who knows the way
The spell that binds the earth and sky

He is the one who seeks the power
The glory of the immortal life
He is the one who waits the hour
The moment of the final strife

He is the enemy of the living kind
The sorcerer, the hopping head
He is the source of the evil mind
That rules the stiff corpses of the lore

Live A Life : An Epicurean Life

When life becomes a living hell
And every breath is filled with pain
When hope is lost and dreams are quelled
And nothing seems to be in vain

Do not despair or curse your fate

Do not give up or turn around
Do not succumb to fear or hate
Do not let darkness drag you down

But keep on moving through the fire
And face the demons in your way
And keep on reaching ever higher
And find the light in every day

For hell is not a place to dwell
But a passage to a better self
And every trial is a test
To make you stronger than the rest

And every wound is a scar
To remind you of how far
You have come and who you are
A survivor and a star

And every tear is a seed
To grow a flower from your need
And every smile is a gift
To lift your spirit and uplift

And every word is a song
To sing along and to belong
And every thought is a power
To shape your world and to empower

And every breath is a chance
To live and love and to enhance
And every dream is a vision
To inspire and to envision

And every step is a journey

To explore and to learn
And every end is a new beginning
To create and to earn your better version of yourself

425

Wandering Through The Nights

I have roamed through countless nights of gloom
And faced the shadows of my lonely doom
I have seen the stars fade and the moon wane
And felt the coldness of the cosmic pain
I have searched for meaning in the dark abyss
And found no answer to my soul's distress

I have questioned the purpose of my breath
And wondered if there is life after death
I have walked the path of the unknown
And I have learned to fear no darkness shown

I have witnessed the beauty of the dawn
And marveled at the light that always shone
I have heard the music of the birds
And felt the joy that fills their simple words
I have touched the flowers of the earth
And sensed the power of their silent worth
I have tasted the sweetness of the rain
And savored the freshness of its stain
I have smelled the fragrance of the breeze
And breathed the essence of its mysterics
I have lived the gift of the present
And I have learned to love the light that's sent

I have explored the wonders of the world
And traveled to the places where they're hurled
I have met the people of different lands
And learned to respect their diverse stands
I have seen the cultures of the east
And admired the richness of their feast
I have experienced the ways of the west
And appreciated the freedom of their quest
I have embraced the values of the south
And honored the warmth of their mouth
I have discovered the secrets of the north
And followed the wisdom of their forth
I have enjoyed the diversity of the planet
And I have learned to cherish the life that's in it

I have faced the challenges of the times
And struggled to overcome their crimes

I have witnessed the horrors of the wars
And mourned the losses of their scars
I have seen the injustices of the systems
And fought the oppressions of their symptoms
I have heard the cries of the poor
And helped the needs of their cure
I have felt the pains of the sick
And shared the hopes of their trick
I have known the sorrows of the lonely
And offered the comforts of my company
I have endured the hardships of the human
And I have learned to be compassionate to every man

I have dreamed the visions of the future
And imagined the possibilities of their nature
I have seen the wonders of the science
And marveled at the achievements of their alliance
I have heard the promises of the technology
And anticipated the benefits of their ecology
I have felt the potentials of the art
And admired the expressions of their heart
I have known the joys of the creativity
And celebrated the diversity of their activity
I have tasted the delights of the innovation
And appreciated the challenges of their creation
I have lived the excitement of the progress
And I have learned to embrace the change that's in excess

I have questioned the limits of the reason
And explored the boundaries of their season
I have seen the paradoxes of the logic
And puzzled over the mysteries of their magic
I have heard the riddles of the language
And deciphered the meanings of their message
I have felt the contradictions of the emotion

And balanced the extremes of their motion
I have known the complexities of the mind
And understood the simplicities of their kind
I have tasted the subtleties of the intuition
And trusted the insights of their vision
I have lived the adventure of the thought
And I have learned to respect the truth that's sought

I have sensed the presence of the spirit
And connected with the essence of their merit
I have seen the radiance of the soul
And felt the brightness of their whole
I have heard the harmony of the music
And joined the melody of their lyric
I have touched the tenderness of the love
And shared the gentleness of their dove
I have known the peace of the meditation
And experienced the bliss of their elevation
I have tasted the sweetness of the joy
And savored the lightness of their toy
I have lived the beauty of the being
And I have learned to appreciate the grace that's freeing

I have transcended the boundaries of the self
And expanded the horizons of their shelf
I have seen the unity of the all
And felt the oneness of their call
I have heard the silence of the nothing
And listened to the voice of their everything
I have touched the emptiness of the space
And filled the fullness of their place
I have known the eternity of the time
And lived the infinity of their rhyme
I have tasted the neutrality of the zero
And balanced the polarity of their hero

I have been the mystery of the existence
And I have learned to surrender to the persistence

I have roamed through countless nights of gloom
And faced the shadows of my lonely doom
But I have also seen the light of the day
And felt the warmth of their ray
I have searched for meaning in the dark abyss
But I have also found the answer in their bliss
I have questioned the purpose of my breath
But I have also wondered at the miracle of their death
I have walked the path of the unknown
But I have also learned to trust the guidance of their shown
I have wandered a thousand midnights
But I have also lived a thousand sunlights

Breaking the Rules: A Poet's Joy

Poetry is the craft of listening to the silence
And transcribing its whispers on the page
It is the skill of discerning the hidden meaning
Behind the words that people often say

Poetry is the quest of exploring the unknown

And mapping its contours with the pen
It is the journey of discovering the self
Beyond the roles that we play for them

Poetry is the voice of expressing the truth
And challenging the lies that we are told
It is the power of creating the beauty
From the chaos that we behold

Poetry is the art of feeling the emotions
And conveying them with the rhyme
It is the gift of sharing the experiences
That transcend the boundaries of time

Poetry is the act of questioning the reality
And imagining the alternatives that could be
It is the vision of seeing the potential
That others often fail to see

Poetry is the way of connecting with the others
And finding the common ground that we share
It is the bond of building the empathy
That shows that we truly care

Poetry is the joy of playing with the language
And finding the words that fit the best
It is the fun of experimenting with the form
And breaking the rules that limit the rest

Poetry is the passion of pursuing the excellence
And honing the craft with every day
It is the dedication of committing to the work
And not giving up along the way

Poetry is the life of living with the purpose

And finding the meaning in the words
It is the love of doing what we love
And writing it down for the world

433

The Fading of All That Matters

Without her smile, the days are long
And life seems like a barren land
Where nothing grows and all is wrong
And hope is buried in the sand

Without her smile, the nights are cold

And dreams are haunted by her face
Where memories stir and pain takes hold
And sleep is lost in endless chase

Without her smile, the world is dull
And colors fade to shades of gray
Where beauty fades and joy is null
And nothing matters anyway

Without her smile, the self is lost
And identity is hard to find
Where purpose wanes and values cost
And meaning is left far behind

Without her smile, the heart is numb
And feelings are a distant past
Where love is dead and passion dumb
And nothing ever seems to last

Without her smile, the soul is dark
And faith is but a hollow word
Where doubt prevails and fear leaves mark
And nothing sacred is preferred

Without her smile, the mind is weak
And thoughts are scattered and confused
Where logic fails and reason bleak
And nothing makes the slightest sense

Without her smile, the spirit is low
And energy is hard to muster
Where motivation ebbs and flow
And nothing sparks the slightest luster

Without her smile, the life is vain

And existence is a curse to bear
Where happiness is out of reach
And nothing else can ever compare

The Last Breath of Love

She is the sole verse of breath in my chest
And I will keep it till the heavens burst
And all the light is swallowed by the night
That quenches the flame of my love for her

She is the lone rhyme of hope in my heart

And I will guard it till the earth is torn
And all the life is shattered by the strife
That rends the bond of my faith in her

She is the only song of joy in my soul
And I will sing it till the seas are dry
And all the sound is silenced by the ground
That buries the voice of my praise for her

She is the unique word of truth in my mind
And I will speak it till the skies are mute
And all the thought is frozen by the cold
That numbs the sense of my trust in her

She is the rare dream of beauty in my eyes
And I will see it till the suns are blind
And all the sight is darkened by the night
That dims the vision of my awe for her

She is the precious gem of grace in my hands
And I will hold it till the stars are dust
And all the touch is broken by the rust
That corrodes the feeling of my care for her

She is the sweet scent of love in my nose
And I will smell it till the flowers are dead
And all the smell is spoiled by the hell
That burns the fragrance of my passion for her

She is the fine taste of bliss in my mouth
And I will savor it till the fruits are gone
And all the taste is bittered by the waste
That poisons the delight of my desire for her

She is the sublime sense of life in my being

And I will live it till the end of time
And all the meaning is lost in the void
That empties the purpose of my existence for her

Gracias

Dear Reader,

As you close the pages on the latest installment in Mawphniang Napoleon's celebrated Homo Sapiens anthology series, we wanted to extend our deepest thanks. Without devoted readers like yourself, Napoleon's decades-long mission of connecting humanity through poetry would not be possible.

Whether you are a longtime fan who has grown alongside this series or a newcomer discovering Napoleon's gifts for the first time, we are humbled you chose to go on this journey with us. We hope you found within these carefully curated verses the transporting magic that only poetry can provide. That they awakened you to new voices while reconnecting you to masters of eras past. That they gifted you moments of consolation, joy, insight and awe.

Most of all, we hope this thoughtful collection illuminated our shared human spirit across borders and time. As Napoleon assembled these contemporary works, he held you in his mind's eye - fellow travelers seeking resonance in poetry's mirror. Kindred spirits united by verse despite life's surface differences.

Thank you for continuing on this literary voyage with Napoleon as your guide. Your readership empowers him to keep shining light on poetry's diverse and timeless gifts. We look forward to having you aboard for the next installation. But for now, fare thee well, until we meet again between pages.

With Gratitude,
The Homo Sapiens Series Team

Note :

As I, a breviloquent raptor, wield A lever, with naught else to my design, I generate tones for the aural field In this prosaic orb we call mankind. My actions, though, are but a small part Of forces far beyond my control, For nature holds the key to each chart And sets the laws that govern the whole. But still, I am compelled to explore The workings of this vast machinery, To seek the truth that lies at core And find the answers to humanity. Though some may call it quest I'll seek the truth, with no time to rest.

About The Poet

PC : Clarissa Candace Giri K

Mawphniang Napoleon, a man of myriad passions, brings his boundless curiosity and verve to all his endeavors. Though a lawyer and entrepreneur by trade, he is a writer and humanist at heart. Ever-striving and unresting, Napoleon embraces new ideas with an open mind. He ventures boldly into uncharted territory, seeking to wring from life all it has to offer. His inquisitive spirit knows no bounds as he delves into existential enigmas. Yet he also finds joy in small moments, cherishing each instant of his journey of self-discovery. Napoleon makes the most of time's fleeting sands, fearlessly writing his story with zest and zeal. Originally from the village of Syadheh in Meghalaya's Ri Bhoi District, India, he exemplifies the region's values of adventure and living life to the fullest.

Note

The newest addition to Mawphniang Napoleon's beloved Homo Sapiens anthology series is here - 121 contemporary poems expertly curated to speak to the soul of verse devotees.

Within these pages, longtime fans will discover fresh voices alongside reconnections with masters past. And newcomers will find a profoundly moving introduction to poetry's transporting power.

Napoleon's profound discernment and passion shine through in every carefully chosen work - reaffirming his peerless status among modern curators. This magical volume has something for every poetry lover, from those who've collected all 17 previous installments to those just discovering Napoleon's gifts.

Lose yourself in lyrical landscapes of joy, grief, wonder and insight. Emerge renewed, reminded of our shared humanity.

For anyone seeking magic, solace and community through verse, the Homo Sapiens series is a must-read. Add the transporting Part XVIII to your collection today and discover Napoleon's poetic sorcery for yourself!

Regards

The Homo Sapiens Series Team

Thank You

With Love and Hugs

www.ingramcontent.com/pod-product-compliance
Lightning Source LLC
Chambersburg PA
CBHW031952150726
47990CB00005B/1671